THE SILVER BOX

A Comedy in Three Acts

JOHN GALSWORTHY

With school and acting notes by
JOHN HAMPDEN, M.A.

DUCKWORTH

This impression 1977
First published 1911
Thirty-second impression 1962
This edition 1964
Reprinted in larger format 1977

Gerald Duckworth & Co. Ltd.
The Old Piano Factory
43 Gloucester Crescent, London N.W.1

ISBN 0 7156 1227 1 (cased)
0 7156 1228 X (paper)

*First performed at
the Court Theatre, London
on September 25th, 1906*

Printed in Great Britain by
Unwin Brothers Limited
The Gresham Press, Old Woking, Surrey

THE SILVER BOX

A Comedy in Three Acts

CONTENTS

CHARACTERS OF THE PLAY

JOHN BARTHWICK, M.P., *a wealthy Liberal*
MRS. BARTHWICK, *his wife*
JACK BARTHWICK, *their son*
ROPER, *their solicitor*
MRS. JONES, *their charwoman*
MARLOW, *their manservant*
WHEELER, *their maidservant*
JONES, *the stranger within their gates*
MRS. SEDDON, *a landlady*
SNOW, *a detective*
A POLICE MAGISTRATE
AN UNKNOWN LADY, *from beyond*
TWO LITTLE GIRLS, *homeless*
LIVENS, *their father*
A RELIEVING OFFICER
A MAGISTRATE'S CLERK
AN USHER
POLICEMEN, CLERKS, AND OTHERS

TIME: The present (1906). The action of the first two Acts takes place on Easter Tuesday; the action of the third on Wednesday of the following week.

ACT I, SCENE I. London, Rockingham Gate. John Barthwick's dining-room.
    SCENE II. The same.
    SCENE III. The same.

ACT II, SCENE I. The Joneses' lodgings, Merthyr Street.
    SCENE II. John Barthwick's dining-room.

ACT III. A London police court.

ACT I

SCENE I

The curtain rises on the BARTHWICKS' *dining-room, large, modern, and well furnished; the window curtains drawn. Electric light is burning. On the large round dining-table is set out a tray with whisky, a syphon, and a silver cigarette-box. It is past midnight.*

A fumbling is heard outside the door. It is opened suddenly; JACK BARTHWICK *seems to fall into the room. He stands holding by the door knob, staring before him, with a beatific smile. He is in evening dress and opera hat, and carries in his hand a sky-blue velvet lady's reticule. His boyish face is freshly coloured and clean-shaven. An overcoat is hanging on his arm.*

JACK. Hallo! I've got home all ri—— [*Defiantly.*] Who says I sh'd never've opened th' door without 'sistance. [*He staggers in, fumbling with the reticule. A lady's handkerchief and purse of crimson silk fall out.*] Serve her joll' well right—everything droppin' out. Th' cat. I've scored her off—I've got her bag. [*He swings the reticule.*] Serves her joll' well right. [*He takes a cigarette out of the silver box and puts it in his mouth.*] Never gave tha' fellow anything! [*He hunts through all his pockets and pulls a shilling out; it drops and rolls away. He looks for it.*] Beastly shilling! [*He looks again.*] Base ingratitude! Absolutely nothing. [*He laughs.*] Mus' tell him I've got absolutely nothing.

[*He lurches through the door and down a corridor, and presently returns, followed by* JONES, *who is advanced in liquor.* JONES, *about thirty years of age, has hollow cheeks, black circles round his eyes, and rusty clothes. He looks as though he might be unemployed, and enters in a hang-dog manner.*]

3

JACK. Sh! sh! sh! Don't you make a noise, whatever you do. Shu' the door, an' have a drink. [*Very solemnly.*] You helped me to open the door—I've got nothin' for you. This is my house. My father's name's Barthwick; he's Member of Parliament—Liberal Member of Parliament: I've told you that before. Have a drink! [*He pours out whisky and drinks it up.*] I'm not drunk—— [*Subsiding on a sofa.*] Tha's all right. Wha's your name? My name's Barthwick, so's my father's; *I'm* a Liberal too—wha're you?

JONES. [*In a thick, sardonic voice*] I'm a bloomin' Conservative. My name's Jones! My wife works 'ere; she's the char; she works 'ere.

JACK. Jones? [*He laughs.*] There's 'nother Jones at college with me. I'm not a Socialist myself; I'm a Liberal—there's ve-lill difference, because of the principles of the Lib—Liberal Party. We're all equal before the law—tha's rot, tha's silly. [*Laughs.*] Wha' was I about to say? Give me some whisky. [JONES *gives him the whisky he desires, together with a squirt of syphon.*] Wha' I was goin' tell you was—I've had a row with her. [*He waves the reticule.*] Have a drink, Jones—sh'd never have got in without you—tha's why I'm giving you a drink. Don' care who knows I've scored her off. Th' cat! [*He throws his feet up on the sofa.*] Don' you make a noise, whatever you do. You pour out a drink—you make yourself good long, long drink—you take cigarette—you take anything you like. Sh'd never have got in without you. [*Closing his eyes.*] You're a Tory—you're a Tory Socialist. I'm Liberal myself—have a drink—I'm an excel'nt chap.

[*His head drops back. He, smiling, falls asleep, and* JONES *stands looking at him; then, snatching up* JACK'S *glass, he drinks it off. He picks the reticule from off* JACK'S *shirt-front, holds it to the light, and smells at it.*]

JONES. Been on the tiles and brought 'ome some of yer cat's fur. [*He stuffs it into* JACK'S *breast pocket.*]

JACK. [*Murmuring*] I've scored you off! You cat!

[JONES *looks around him furtively; he pours out whisky and drinks it. From the silver box he takes a cigarette, puffs at it, and drinks more whisky. There is no sobriety left in him.*

JONES. Fat lot o' things they've got 'ere! [*He sees the crimson purse lying on the floor.*] More cat's fur. Puss, puss! [*He fingers it, drops it on the tray, and looks at* JACK.] Calf! Fat calf! [*He sees his own presentment in a mirror. Lifting his hands, with fingers spread, he stares at it; then looks again at* JACK, *clenching his fist as if to batter in his sleeping, smiling face. Suddenly he tilts the rest of the whisky into the glass and drinks it. With cunning glee he takes the silver box and purse and pockets them.*] I'll score *you* off too, that's wot I'll do!

[*He gives a little snarling laugh and lurches to the door. His shoulder rubs against the switch; the light goes out. There is a sound as of a closing outer door.*]

The curtain falls.
The curtain rises again at once.

SCENE II

In the BARTHWICKS' *dining-room.* JACK *is still asleep; the morning light is coming through the curtains. The time is half-past eight.* WHEELER, *brisk person, enters with a dust-pan, and* MRS. JONES *more slowly with a scuttle.*

WHEELER. [*Drawing the curtains*] That precious husband of yours was round for you after you'd gone yesterday, Mrs. Jones. Wanted your money for drink, I suppose. He hangs about the corner here half the time. I saw him outside the "Goat and Bells" when I went to the post last night. If I were you I wouldn't live with him. I wouldn't live with a man that raised his hand to me. I wouldn't put up with it. Why don't you take the children and leave him? If you put up with 'im it'll only make him worse. I never can see why, because a man's married you, he should knock you about.

MRS. JONES. [*Slim, dark-eyed, and dark-haired; oval-faced, and with a smooth, soft, even voice; her manner patient, her way of talking quite impersonal; she wears a blue linen dress, and boots with holes*] It was nearly two last night before he come home, and he wasn't himself. He made me get up, and he knocked me about; he didn't seem to know *what* he was saying or doing. Of course I *would* leave him, but I'm really afraid of what he'd do to me. He's such a violent man when he's not himself.

WHEELER. Why don't you get him locked up? You'll never have any peace until you get him locked up. If I were you I'd go to the police court to-morrow. That's what I would do.

MRS. JONES. Of course I ought to go, because he does treat me so badly when he's not himself. But you see, Bettina, he has a very hard time—he's been out of work two months, and it preys upon his mind. When he's in work he behaves himself much better. It's when he's out of work that he's so violent.

WHEELER. Well, if you won't take any steps you'll never get rid of him.

MRS. JONES. Of course it's very wearing to me; I don't get my sleep at nights. And it's not as if I were getting help from him, because I have to do for the children and all of us. And he throws such dreadful things up at me, talks of my having men to follow me about. Such a thing never happens; no man ever speaks to me. And of course it's just the other way. It's what he does that's wrong and makes me so unhappy. And then he's always threatenin' to cut my throat if I leave him. It's all the drink, and things preying on his mind; he's not a bad man really. Sometimes he'll speak quite kind to me, but I've stood so much from him, I don't feel it in me to speak kind back, but just keep myself to myself. And he's all right with the children too, except when he's not himself.

WHEELER. You mean when he's drunk, the beauty.

MRS. JONES. Yes. [*Without change of voice.*] There's the young gentleman asleep on the sofa.

[*They both look silently at* JACK.

MRS. JONES. [*At last, in her soft voice*] He doesn't look quite himself.

WHEELER. He's a young limb, that what he is. It's my belief he was tipsy last night, like your husband. It's another kind of bein' out of work that sets *him* to drink. I'll go and tell Marlow. This is his job. [*She goes.*

[MRS. JONES, *upon her knees, begins a gentle sweeping.*

JACK. [*Waking*] Who's there? What is it?

MRS. JONES. It's me, sir, Mrs. Jones.

JACK. [*Sitting up and looking round*] Where is it—what— what time is it?

MRS. JONES. It's getting on for nine o'clock, sir.

JACK. For nine! Why—what! [*Rising, and loosening his tongue; putting hand to his head, and staring hard at* MRS. JONES.] Look here, you, Mrs.—Mrs. Jones—don't you say you caught me asleep here.

MRS. JONES. No, sir, of course I won't, sir.

JACK. It's quite an accident; I don't know how it happened. I must have forgotten to go to bed. It's a queer thing. I've got a most beastly headache. Mind you don't say anything, Mrs. Jones.

[*Goes out and passes* MARLOW *in the doorway.* MARLOW *is young and quiet; he is clean-shaven, and his hair is brushed high from his forehead in a coxcomb. Incidentally a butler, he is first a man. He looks at* MRS. JONES, *and smiles a private smile.*

MARLOW. Not the first time, and won't be the last. Looked a bit dicky, eh, Mrs. Jones?

MRS. JONES. He didn't look quite himself. Of course I didn't take notice.

MARLOW. You're used to them. How's your old man?

MRS. JONES. [*Softly as throughout*] Well, he was very bad last night; he didn't seem to know what he was about. He was very late, and he was most abusive. But now, of course, he's asleep.

MARLOW. That's his way of finding a job, eh?

MRS. JONES. As a rule, Mr. Marlow, he goes out early every morning looking for work, and sometimes he comes in fit to drop—and of course I can't say he doesn't try to get it, because he does. Trade's very bad. [*She stands quite still, her pan and brush before her, at the beginning and the end of long vistas of experience, traversing them with her impersonal eye.*] But he's not a good husband to me—last night he hit me, and he was so dreadfully abusive.

MARLOW. Bank 'oliday, eh! He's too fond of the "Goat and Bells," that's what's the matter with him. I see him at the corner late every night. He hangs about.

MRS. JONES. He gets to feeling very low walking about all day after work, and being refused so often, and then when he gets a drop in him it goes to his head. But he shouldn't treat his wife as he treats me. Sometimes I've had to go and walk about at night, when he wouldn't let me stay in the room; but he's sorry for it afterwards. And he hangs about after me, he waits for me in the street; and I don't think he ought to, because I've always been a good wife to him. And I tell him Mrs. Barthwick wouldn't like him coming about the place. But that only makes him angry, and he says dreadful things about the gentry. Of course it was through me that he first lost his place, through his not treating me right; and that's made him bitter against the gentry. He had a very good place as groom in the country; but it made such a stir, because of course he didn't treat me right.

MARLOW. Got the sack?

MRS. JONES. Yes; his employer said he couldn't keep him, because there was a great deal of talk; and he said it was such a bad example. But it's very important for me to keep my work here; I have the three children, and I don't want him to come about after me in the streets, and make a disturbance as he sometimes does.

MARLOW. [*Holding up the empty decanter*] Not a drain! Next time he hits you get a witness and go down to the court——

MRS. JONES. Yes, I think I've made up my mind. I think I ought to.

MARLOW. That's right. Where's the ciga——? [*He*

searches for the silver box; he looks at Mrs. Jones, *who is sweeping on her hands and knees; he checks himself and stands reflecting. From the tray he picks two half-smoked cigarettes, and reads the name of them.*] Nestor—where the deuce——?

[*With a meditative air he looks again at* Mrs. Jones, *and, taking up* Jack's *overcoat, he searches in the pockets.* Wheeler, *with a tray of breakfast things, comes in.*

Marlow.   [*Aside to* Wheeler] Have you seen the cigarette-box?

Wheeler.   No.

Marlow.   Well, it's gone.   I put it on the tray last night. And he's been smoking [*Showing her the ends of cigarette.*] It's not in these pockets.   He can't have taken it upstairs this morning!   Have a good look in his room when he comes down. Who's been in here?

Wheeler.   Only me and Mrs. Jones.

Mrs. Jones.   I've finished here;   shall I do the drawing-room now?

Wheeler.   [*Looking at her doubtfully*] Have you seen—— Better do the boudwower first.

[Mrs. Jones *goes out with pan and brush.* Marlow *and* Wheeler *look each other in the face.*

Marlow.   It'll turn up.

Wheeler.   [*Hesitating*] You don't think *she*—— [*Nodding at the door.*]

Marlow.   [*Stoutly*] I don't—I never believes anything of anybody.

Wheeler.   But the master'll have to be told.

Marlow.   You wait a bit, and see if it don't turn up. Suspicion's no business of ours.   I set my mind against it.

The curtain falls.

The curtain rises again at once.

SCENE III

BARTHWICK *and* MRS. BARTHWICK *are seated at the breakfast table. He is a man between fifty and sixty; quietly important, with a bald forehead, and pince-nez, and "The Times" in his hand. She is a lady of nearly fifty, well dressed, with greyish hair, good features, and a decided manner. They face each other.*

BARTHWICK. [*From behind his paper*] The Labour man has got in at the by-election for Barnside, my dear.

MRS. BARTHWICK. Another Labour? I can't think what on earth the country is about.

BARTHWICK. I predicted it. It's not a matter of vast importance.

MRS. BARTHWICK. Not? How can you take it so calmly, John? To me it's simply outrageous. And there you sit, you Liberals, and pretend to encourage these people!

BARTHWICK. [*Frowning*] The representation of all parties is necessary for any proper reform, for any proper social policy.

MRS. BARTHWICK. I've no patience with your talk of reform—all that nonsense about social policy. We know perfectly well what it is they want; they want things for themselves. Those Socialists and Labour men are an absolutely selfish set of people. They have no sense of patriotism, like the upper classes, *they simply want what we've got.*

BARTHWICK. Want what we've got! [*He stares into space.*] My dear, what are you talking about? [*With a contortion.*] I'm no alarmist.

MRS. BARTHWICK. Cream? Quite uneducated men! Wait until they begin to tax our investments. I'm convinced that when they once get a chance they will tax everything—they've no feeling for the country. You Liberals and Conservatives, you're all alike; you don't see an inch before your noses.

You've no imagination, not a scrap of imagination between you. You ought to join hands and nip it in the bud.

BARTHWICK.   You're talking nonsense!   How is it possible for Liberals and Conservatives to join hands, as you call it? That shows how absurd it is for women—— Why, the very essence of a Liberal is to trust in the people!

MRS. BARTHWICK.   Now, John, eat your breakfast.   As if there were any real difference between you and the Conservatives.   All the upper classes have the same interests to protect, and the same principles.   [*Calmly.*]   Oh! you're sitting upon a volcano, John.

BARTHWICK.   What!

MRS. BARTHWICK.   I read a letter in the paper yesterday. I forget the man's name, but it made the whole thing perfectly clear.   You don't look things in the face.

BARTHWICK.   Indeed!   [*Heavily.*]   I am a Liberal.   Drop the subject, please!

MRS. BARTHWICK.   Toast?   I quite agree with what this man says: Education is simply ruining the lower classes.   It unsettles them, and that's the worst thing for us all.   I see an enormous difference in the manner of servants.

BARTHWICK.   [*With suspicious emphasis*]   I welcome any change that will lead to something better.   [*He opens a letter.*] H'm!   This is that affair of Master Jack's again.   "High Street, Oxford.   Sir, We have received Mr. John Barthwick, Senior's, draft for forty pounds."   Oh! the letter's to him! "We now enclose the cheque you cashed with us, which, as we stated in our previous letter, was not met on presentation at your bank.   We are, Sir, yours obediently, Moss and Sons, Tailors." H'm!   [*Staring at the cheque.*]   A pretty business altogether! The boy might have been prosecuted.

MRS. BARTHWICK.   Come, John, you know Jack didn't mean anything; he only thought he was overdrawing.   I still think his bank ought to have cashed that cheque.   They must know your position.

BARTHWICK.   [*Replacing in the envelope the letter and the cheque*] Much good that would have done him in a court of law. [*He stops as* JACK *comes in, fastening his waistcoat and staunching a razor cut upon his chin.*]

JACK. [*Sitting down between them, and speaking with an artificial joviality*] Sorry I'm late. [*He looks lugubriously at the dishes.*] Tea, please, mother. Any letters for me? [BARTH-WICK *hands the letter to him.*] But look here, I say, this has been opened! I do wish you wouldn't——

BARTHWICK. [*Touching the envelope*] I suppose I'm entitled to this name.

JACK. [*Sulkily*] Well, I can't help having your name, father! [*He reads the letter, and mutters.*] Brutes.

BARTHWICK. [*Eyeing him*] You don't deserve to be so well out of that.

JACK. Haven't you ragged me enough, dad?

MRS. BARTHWICK. Yes, John, let Jack have his breakfast.

BARTHWICK. If you hadn't had me to come to, where would you have been? It's the merest accident—suppose you had been the son of a poor man or a clerk. Obtaining money with a cheque you knew your bank could not meet. It might have ruined you for life. I can't see what's to become of you if these are your principles. I never did anything of the sort myself.

JACK. I expect you always had lots of money. If you've got plenty of money, of course——

BARTHWICK. On the contrary, I had not your advantages. My father kept me very short of money.

JACK. How much had you, dad?

BARTHWICK. It's not material. The question is, do you feel the gravity of what you did?

JACK. I don't know about the gravity. Of course, I'm very sorry if you think it was wrong. Haven't I said so! I should never have done it at all if I hadn't been so jolly hard up.

BARTHWICK. How much of that forty pounds have you got left, Jack?

JACK. [*Hesitating*] I don't know—not much.

BARTHWICK. How much?

JACK. [*Desperately*] I haven't got any.

BARTHWICK. What?

JACK. I know I've got the most beastly headache.

[*He leans his head on his hand.*

MRS. BARTHWICK. Headache? My dear boy! Can't you eat any breakfast?

JACK. [*Drawing in his breath*] Too jolly bad!

MRS. BARTHWICK. I'm so sorry. Come with me, dear; I'll give you something that will take it away at once.

[*They leave the room; and* BARTHWICK, *tearing up the letter, goes to the fireplace and puts the pieces in the fire. While he is doing this* MARLOW *comes in, and, looking round him, is about quietly to withdraw.*

BARTHWICK. What's that? What d'you want?

MARLOW. I was looking for Mr. John, sir.

BARTHWICK. What d'you want Mr. John for?

MARLOW. [*With hesitation*] I thought I should find him here, sir.

BARTHWICK. [*Suspiciously*] Yes, but what do you want him for?

MARLOW. [*Offhandedly*] There's a lady called—asked to speak to him for a minute, sir.

BARTHWICK. A lady, at this time of the morning. What sort of a lady?

MARLOW. [*Without expression in his voice*] I can't tell, sir; no particular sort. She might be after charity. She might be a Sister of Mercy, I should think, sir.

BARTHWICK. Is she dressed like one?

MARLOW. No, sir, she's in plain clothes, sir.

BARTHWICK. Didn't she say what she wanted?

MARLOW. No, sir.

BARTHWICK. Where did you leave her?

MARLOW. In the hall, sir.

BARTHWICK. In the hall? How do you know she's not a thief—not got designs on the house?

MARLOW. No, sir, I don't fancy so, sir.

BARTHWICK. Well, show her in here; I'll see her myself.

[MARLOW *goes out with a private gesture of dismay. He soon returns, ushering in a young pale lady with dark eyes and pretty figure, in a modish, black, but rather shabby dress, a black and white trimmed hat with a bunch of Parma violets wrongly placed, and fuzzy-spotted veil. At the sight of* MR. BARTHWICK *she exhibits every sign of nervousness.* MARLOW *goes out.*

UNKNOWN LADY. Oh! but—I beg pardon—there's some mistake—I—— [*She turns to fly.*]

BARTHWICK. Whom did you want to see, madam?

UNKNOWN. [*Stopping and looking back*] It was Mr. *John* Barthwick I wanted to see.

BARTHWICK. I am John Barthwick, madam. What can I have the pleasure of doing for you?

UNKNOWN. Oh! I—I don't—— [*She drops her eyes.* BARTHWICK *scrutinizes her, and purses his lips.*]

BARTHWICK. It was my son, perhaps, you wished to see?

UNKNOWN. [*Quickly*] Yes, of course, it's your son.

BARTHWICK. May I ask whom I have the pleasure of speaking to?

UNKNOWN. [*Appeal and hardiness upon her face*] My name is—oh! it doesn't matter—I don't want to make any fuss. I just want to see your son for a minute. [*Boldly.*] In fact, I *must* see him.

BARTHWICK. [*Controlling his uneasiness*] My son is not very well. If necessary, no doubt I could attend to the matter; be so kind as to let me know——

UNKNOWN. Oh! but I *must* see him—I've come on purpose—— [*She bursts out nervously.*] I don't want to make any fuss, but the fact is, last—last night your son took away—he took away my—— [*She stops.*

BARTHWICK. [*Severely*] Yes, madam, what?

UNKNOWN. He took away my—my reticule.

BARTHWICK. Your reti——?

UNKNOWN. I don't care about the reticule; it's not *that*

I want—I'm sure I don't want to make any fuss—[*her face is quivering*]—but—but—all my money was in it!

BARTHWICK. In what—in what?

UNKNOWN. In my purse, in the reticule. It was a crimson silk purse. Really, I wouldn't have come—I don't want to make any fuss. But I must get my money back—mustn't I?

BARTHWICK. Do you tell me that my son——?

UNKNOWN. Oh! well, you see, he wasn't quite—I mean he was—— [*She smiles mesmerically.*

BARTHWICK. I beg your pardon.

UNKNOWN. [*Stamping her foot*] Oh! don't you see—tipsy! We had a quarrel.

BARTHWICK. [*Scandalized*] How? Where?

UNKNOWN. [*Defiantly*] At my place. We'd had supper at the—— and your son——

BARTHWICK. [*Pressing the bell*] May I ask how you knew this house? Did he give you his name and address?

UNKNOWN. [*Glancing sidelong*] I got it out of his overcoat.

BARTHWICK. [*Sardonically*] Oh! you got it out of his overcoat. And may I ask if my son will know you by daylight?

UNKNOWN. Know me? I should jolly—I mean, of course he will! [MARLOW *comes in.*

BARTHWICK. Ask Mr. John to come down.

[MARLOW *goes out, and* BARTHWICK *walks uneasily about.* And how long have you enjoyed his acquaintanceship?

UNKNOWN. Only since—only since Good Friday.

BARTHWICK. I am at a loss—I repeat I am at a loss——

[*He glances at this unknown lady, who stands with eyes cast down, twisting her hands. And suddenly* JACK *appears. He stops on seeing who is here, and the unknown lady hysterically giggles. There is a silence.*

BARTHWICK. [*Portentously*] This young—er—lady says that last night—I think you said last night, madam—you took away——

UNKNOWN. [*Impulsively*] My reticule, and all my money was in a crimson silk purse.

JACK.   Reticule.   [*Looking round for any chance to get away.*] I don't know anything about it.

BARTHWICK.   [*Sharply*] Come, do you deny seeing this young lady last night?

JACK.   Deny?   No, of course.   [*Whispering*] Why did you give me away like this?   What on earth did you come here for?

UNKNOWN.   [*Tearfully*] I'm sure I didn't want to—it's not likely, is it?   You snatched it out of my hand—you know you did—and the purse had all my money in it.   I didn't follow you last night because I didn't want to make a fuss and it was so late, and you were so——

BARTHWICK.   Come, sir, don't turn your back on me—explain!

JACK.   [*Desperately*] I don't remember anything about it. [*In a low voice to his friend*] Why on earth couldn't you have written?

UNKNOWN.   [*Sullenly*] I want it now; I must have it—I've got to pay my rent to-day.   [*She looks at* BARTHWICK.] They're only too glad to jump on people who are not—not *well off.*

JACK.   I don't remember anything about it, really I don't remember anything about last night at all.   [*He puts his hand up to his head.*]   It's all—cloudy, and I've got such a beastly headache.

UNKNOWN.   But you *took* it; you know you did.   You said you'd score me off.

JACK.   Well, then, it must be here.   I remember now—I remember something.   Why did I take the beastly thing?

BARTHWICK.   Yes, why did you take the beastly——
                              [*He turns abruptly to the window.*

UNKNOWN.   [*With her mesmeric smile*] You weren't quite ——were you?

JACK.   [*Smiling pallidly*] I'm *awfully* sorry.   If there's anything I can do——

BARTHWICK.   Do?   You can restore this property, I suppose.

JACK. I'll go and have a look, but I really don't think I've got it.

[*He goes out hurriedly. And* BARTHWICK, *placing a chair, motions to the visitor to sit; then, with pursed lips, he stands and eyes her fixedly. She sits, and steals a look at him; then turns away, and, drawing up her veil, stealthily wipes her eyes. And* JACK *comes back.*

JACK. [*Ruefully holding out the empty reticule*] Is that the thing? I've looked all over—I can't find the purse anywhere. Are you sure it was there?

UNKNOWN. [*Tearfully*] Sure? Of course I'm sure. A crimson silk purse. It was all the money I had.

JACK. I really am awfully sorry—my head's so jolly bad. I've asked the butler, but he hasn't seen it.

UNKNOWN. I *must* have my money——

JACK. Oh! Of course—that'll be all right; I'll see that that's all right. How much?

UNKNOWN. [*Sullenly*] Seven pounds—twelve—it's all I've got in the world.

JACK. That'll be all right; I'll—send you a—cheque.

UNKNOWN. [*Eagerly*] No; now, please. Give me what was in my purse; I've got to pay my rent this morning. They won't give me another day; I'm a fortnight behind already.

JACK. [*Blankly*] I'm awfully sorry; I really haven't a penny in my pocket. [*He glances stealthily at* BARTHWICK.

UNKNOWN. [*Excitedly*] Come, I say you must—it's my money, and you took it. I'm not going away without it. They'll turn me out of my place.

JACK. [*Clasping his head*] But I can't give you what I haven't got. Don't I tell you I haven't a beastly penny?

UNKNOWN. [*Tearing at her handkerchief*] Oh! do give it me! [*She puts her hands together in appeal; then, with sudden fierceness.*] If you don't I'll summons you. It's stealing, that's what it is!

BARTHWICK. [*Uneasily*] One moment, please. As a matter of—er—principle, I shall settle this claim. [*He produces*

money.]   Here is eight pounds; the extra will cover the value
of the purse and your cab fares.   I need make no comment—
no thanks are necessary.

[*Touching the bell, he holds the door ajar in silence.   The
unknown lady stores the money in her reticule, she looks from* JACK
to BARTHWICK, *and her face is quivering faintly with a smile.
She hides it with her hand, and steals away.   Behind her*
BARTHWICK *shuts the door.*

BARTHWICK.   [*With solemnity*] H'm!   This is a nice thing
to happen!

JACK.   [*Impersonally*] What awful luck!

BARTHWICK.   So this is the way that forty pounds has gone!
One thing after another!   Once more I should like to know
where you'd have been if it hadn't been for me!   You don't
seem to have any principles.   You—you're one of those who
are a nuisance to society; you—you're dangerous!   What your
mother would say I don't know.   Your conduct, as far as I can
see, is absolutely unjustifiable.   It's—it's criminal.   Why, a
poor man who behaved as you've done . . . d'you think he'd
have any mercy shown him?   What you want is a good lesson.
You and your sort are—[*he speaks with feeling*]—a nuisance to
the community.   Don't ask me to help you next time.   You're
not fit to be helped.

JACK.   [*Turning upon his sire, with unexpected fierceness*] All
right, I won't then, and see how you like it.   You wouldn't
have helped me this time, I know, if you hadn't been scared the
thing would get into the papers.   Where are the cigarettes?

BARTHWICK.   [*Regarding him uneasily*] Well—I'll say no
more about it.   [*He rings the bell.*]   I'll pass it over for this
once, but—— [MARLOW *comes in.*]   You can clear away.
[*He hides his face behind "The Times."*

JACK.   [*Brightening*] I say, Marlow, where are the cigarettes?

MARLOW.   I put the box out with the whisky last night, sir,
but this morning I can't find it anywhere.

JACK.   Did you look in my room?

MARLOW.   Yes, sir; I've looked all over the house.   I

found two Nestor ends in the tray this morning, so you must have been smokin' last night, sir. [*Hesitating.*] I'm really afraid some one's purloined the box.

JACK. [*Uneasily*] Stolen it!

BARTHWICK. What's that? The cigarette-box! Is anything else missing?

MARLOW. No, sir; I've been through the plate.

BARTHWICK. Was the house all right this morning? None of the windows open?

MARLOW. No, sir. [*Quietly to* JACK.] You left your latchkey in the door last night, sir.

[*He hands it back, unseen by* BARTHWICK.

JACK. Tst!

BARTHWICK. Who's been in the room this morning?

MARLOW. Me and Wheeler, and Mrs. Jones is all, sir, as far as I know.

BARTHWICK. Have you asked Mrs. Barthwick? [*To* JACK.] Go and ask your mother if she's had it; ask her to look and see if she's missed anything else. [JACK *goes upon his mission.*] Nothing is more disquieting than losing things like this.

MARLOW. No, sir.

BARTHWICK. Have you any suspicions?

MARLOW. No, sir.

BARTHWICK. This Mrs. JONES—how long has she been working here?

MARLOW. Only this last month, sir.

BARTHWICK. What sort of person?

MARLOW. I don't know much about her, sir; seems a very quiet, respectable woman.

BARTHWICK. Who did the room this morning?

MARLOW. Wheeler and Mrs. Jones, sir.

BARTHWICK. [*With his forefinger upraised*] Now, was this Mrs. Jones in the room alone at any time?

MARLOW. [*Expressionless*] Yes, sir.

BARTHWICK. How do you know that?

MARLOW.   [*Reluctantly*] I found her here, sir.

BARTHWICK.   And has Wheeler been in the room alone?

MARLOW.   No, sir, she's not, sir.   I should say, sir, that Mrs. Jones seems a very honest——

BARTHWICK.   [*Holding up his hand*] I want to know this: Has this Mrs. Jones been here the whole morning?

MARLOW.   Yes, sir—no, sir—she stepped over to the green-grocer's for cook.

BARTHWICK.   H'm!   Is she in the house now?

MARLOW.   Yes, sir.

BARTHWICK.   Very good.   I shall make a point of clearing this up.   On principle I shall make a point of fixing the responsi-bility; it goes to the foundations of security.   In all your interests——

MARLOW.   Yes, sir.

BARTHWICK.   What sort of circumstances is this Mrs. Jones in?   Is her husband in work?

MARLOW.   I believe not, sir.

BARTHWICK.   Very well.   Say nothing about it to anyone. Tell Wheeler not to speak of it, and ask Mrs. Jones to step up here.

MARLOW.   Very good, sir.

[MARLOW *goes out, his face concerned; and* BARTHWICK *stays, his face judicial and a little pleased, as befits a man conducting an inquiry.* MRS. BARTHWICK *and her son come in.*

BARTHWICK.   Well, my dear, you've not seen it, I suppose?

MRS. BARTHWICK.   No.   But what an extraordinary thing, John!   Marlow, of course, is out of the question.   I'm certain none of the maids——   As for cook!

BARTHWICK.   Oh, cook!

MRS. BARTHWICK.   Of course!   It's perfectly detestable to me to suspect anybody.

BARTHWICK.   It is not a question of one's feelings.   It's a question of justice.   On principle——

MRS. BARTHWICK.   I shouldn't be a bit surprised if the

charwoman knew something about it. It was Laura who recommended her.

BARTHWICK. [*Judicially*] I am going to have Mrs. Jones up. Leave it to me; and—er—remember that nobody is guilty until they're proved so. I shall be careful. I have no intention of frightening her; I shall give her every chance. I hear she's in poor circumstances. If we are not able to do much for them we are bound to have the greatest sympathy with the poor. [MRS. JONES *comes in.*] [*Pleasantly*] Oh! good morning, Mrs. Jones.

MRS. JONES. [*Soft, and even, unemphatic*] Good morning, sir! Good morning, ma'am!

BARTHWICK. About your husband—he's not in work, I hear?

MRS. JONES. No, sir; of course he's not in work just now.

BARTHWICK. Then I suppose he's earning nothing.

MRS. JONES. No, sir, he's not earning anything just now, sir.

BARTHWICK. And how many children have you?

MRS. JONES. Three children; but of course they don't eat very much, sir. [*A little silence.*

BARTHWICK. And how old is the eldest?

MRS. JONES. Nine years old, sir.

BARTHWICK. Do they go to school?

MRS. JONES. Yes, sir, they all three go to school every day.

BARTHWICK. [*Severely*] And what about their food when you're out at work.

MRS. JONES. Well, sir, I have to give them their dinner to take with them. Of course I'm not always able to give them anything; sometimes I have to send them without; but my husband is very good about the children when he's in work. But when he's not in work of course he's a very difficult man.

BARTHWICK. He drinks, I suppose?

MRS. JONES. Yes, sir. Of course I can't say he doesn't drink, because he does.

BARTHWICK. And I suppose he takes all your money?

Mrs. Jones.   No, sir, he's very good about my money, except when he's not himself, and then, of course, he treats me very badly.

Barthwick.   Now what is he—your husband?

Mrs. Jones.   By profession, sir, of course he's a groom.

Barthwick.   A groom!   How came he to lose his place?

Mrs. Jones.   He lost his place a long time ago, sir, and he's never had a very long job since; and now, of course, the motor-cars are against him.

Barthwick.   When were you married to him, Mrs. Jones?

Mrs. Jones.   Eight years ago, sir—that was in——

Mrs. Barthwick.   [*Sharply*] Eight?   You said the eldest child was nine.

Mrs. Jones.   Yes, ma'am; of course that was why he lost his place.   He didn't treat me rightly, and of course his employer said he couldn't keep him because of the example.

Barthwick.   You mean he—ahem——

Mrs. Jones.   Yes, sir; and of course after he lost his place he married me.

Mrs. Barthwick.   You actually mean to say you—you were——

Barthwick.   My dear——

Mrs. Barthwick.   [*Indignantly*] How disgraceful!

Barthwick.   [*Hurriedly*] And where are you living now, Mrs. Jones?

Mrs. Jones.   We've not got a home, sir.   Of course we've been obliged to put away most of our things.

Barthwick.   Put your things away!   You mean to—to—er—to pawn them?

Mrs. Jones.   Yes, sir, to put them away.   We're living in Merthyr Street—that is close by here, sir—at No. 34.   We just have the one room.

Barthwick.   And what do you pay a week?

Mrs. Jones.   We pay six shillings a week, sir, for a furnished room.

Barthwick.   And I suppose you're behind in the rent?

MRS. JONES. Yes, sir, we're a little behind in the rent.

BARTHWICK. But *you're* in good work, aren't you?

MRS. JONES. Well, sir, I have a day in Stamford Place, Thursdays. And Mondays and Wednesdays and Fridays I come here. But to-day, of course, is a half-day, because of yesterday's Bank Holiday.

BARTHWICK. I see; four days a week, and you get half a crown a day, is that it?

MRS. JONES. Yes, sir, and my dinner; but sometimes it's only half a day, and that's eighteenpence.

BARTHWICK. And when your husband earns anything he spends it in drink, I suppose?

MRS. JONES. Sometimes he does, sir, and sometimes he gives it to me for the children. Of course he would work if he could get it, sir, but it seems there are a great many people out of work.

BARTHWICK. Ah! Yes. We—er—won't go into that. [*Sympathetically*] And how about your work here? Do you find it hard?

MRS. JONES. Oh! no, sir, not very hard, sir; except, of course, when I don't get my sleep at night.

BARTHWICK. Ah! And you help do all the rooms? And sometimes, I suppose, you go out for cook?

MRS. JONES. Yes, sir.

BARTHWICK. And you've been out this morning?

MRS. JONES. Yes, sir, of course I had to go to the green-grocer's.

BARTHWICK. Exactly. So your husband earns nothing? And he's a bad character.

MRS. JONES. No, sir, I don't say that, sir. I think there's a great deal of good in him; though he does treat me very bad sometimes. And of course I don't like to leave him, but I think I ought to, because really I hardly know how to stay with him. He often raises his hand to me. Not long ago he gave me a blow here [*touches her breast*] and I can feel it now. So I think I ought to leave him, don't *you*, sir?

BARTHWICK.   Ah!   I can't help you there.   It's a very serious thing to leave your husband.   Very serious thing.

MRS. JONES.   Yes, sir, of course I'm afraid of what he might do to me if I were to leave him;   he can be so very violent.

BARTHWICK.   H'm!   Well, that I can't pretend to say anything about.   It's the bad principle I'm speaking of——

MRS. JONES.   Yes, sir;   I know nobody can help me.   I know I must decide for myself, and of course I know that he has a very hard life.   And he's fond of the children, and it's very hard for him to see them going without food.

BARTHWICK.   [*Hastily*] Well—er—thank you, I just wanted to hear about you.   I don't think I need detain you any longer, Mrs.—Jones.

MRS. JONES.   No, sir, thank you, sir.

BARTHWICK.   Good morning, then.

MRS. JONES.   Good morning, sir;   good morning, ma'am.

BARTHWICK.   [*Exchanging glances with his wife*] By the way, Mrs. Jones—I think it is only fair to tell you, a silver cigarette-box—er—is missing.

MRS. JONES.   [*Looking from one face to the other*] I am very sorry, sir.

BARTHWICK.   Yes;   you have not seen it, I suppose?

MRS. JONES.   [*Realizing that suspicion is upon her; with an uneasy movement*] Where was it, sir;   if you please, sir?

BARTHWICK.   [*Evasively*] Where did Marlow say?   Er— in this room, yes, in *this* room.

MRS. JONES.   No, sir, I haven't seen it—of course if I'd seen it I should have noticed it.

BARTHWICK.   [*Giving her a rapid glance*] You—you are sure of that?

MRS. JONES.   [*Impassively*] Yes, sir.   [*With a slow nodding of her head.*]   I have not seen it, and of course I *don't* know where it is.   [*She turns and goes quietly out.*

BARTHWICK.   H'm!

[*The three* BARTHWICKS *avoid each other's glances.*

The curtain falls.

ACT II

SCENE I

The JONES' *lodgings, Merthyr Street, at half-past two o'clock.*
The bare room, with tattered oilcloth and damp, distempered walls,
has an air of tidy wretchedness.   On the bed lies JONES, *half-*
dressed; his coat is thrown across his feet, and muddy boots are
lying on the floor close by.   He is asleep.   The door is opened
and MRS. JONES *comes in, dressed in a pinched black jacket and*
old black sailor hat; she carries a parcel wrapped up in "The
Times."   She puts her parcel down, unwraps an apron, half
a loaf, two onions, three potatoes, and a tiny piece of bacon.
Taking a teapot from the cupboard, she rinses it, shakes into it
some powdered tea out of a screw of paper, puts it on the hearth,
and sitting in a wooden chair quietly begins to cry.

JONES.   [*Stirring and yawning*] That you?   What's the
time?

MRS. JONES.   [*Drying her eyes, and in her usual voice*] Half-
past two.

JONES.   What you back so soon for?

MRS. JONES.   I only had the half-day to-day, Jem.

JONES.   [*On his back, and in a drowsy voice*] Got anything
for dinner?

MRS. JONES.   Mrs. Barthwick's cook gave me a little bit of
bacon.   I'm going to make a stew.   [*She prepares for cooking.*]
There's fourteen shillings owing for rent, James, and of course
I've only got two and fourpence.   They'll be coming for it
to-day.

JONES.   [*Turning towards her on his elbow*] Let 'em come
and find my surprise packet.   I've had enough o' this tryin' for

25

work. Why should I go round and round after a job like a bloomin' squirrel in a cage. "Give us a job, sir"—"Take a man on"—"Got a wife and three children." Sick of it I am! I'd sooner lie here and rot. "Jones, you come and join the demonstration; come and 'old a flag, and listen to the ruddy orators, and go 'ome as empty as you came." There's some that seems to like *that*—the sheep! When I go seekin' for a job now, and sees the brutes lookin' me up an' down, it's like a thousand serpents in me. I'm not arskin' for any treat. A man wants to sweat hisself silly and not allowed—that's a rum start, ain't it? A man wants to sweat his soul out to keep the breath in him and ain't allowed—that's justice—that's freedom and all the rest of it. [*He turns his face towards the wall.*] You're so milky mild; you don't know what goes on inside o' me. I'm done with the silly game. If they want me, let 'em come for me!

[MRS. JONES *stops cooking and stands unmoving at the table.*] I've tried and done with it, I tell you. I've never been afraid of what's before *me*. You mark my words—if you think they've broke my spirit, you're mistook. I'll lie and rot sooner than arsk 'em again. What makes you stand like that—you long-sufferin', Gawd-forsaken image—that's why I can't keep my hands off you. So now you know. Work! You can work, but you haven't the spirit of a louse!

MRS. JONES. [*Quietly*] You talk more wild sometimes when you're yourself, James, than when you're not. If you don't get work, how are we to go on? They won't let us stay here; they're looking to their money to-day, I know.

JONES. I see this Barthwick o' yours every day goin' down to Pawlyment snug and comfortable to talk his silly soul out; an' I see that young calf, his son, swellin' it about, and goin' on the razzle-dazzle. Wot 'ave they done that makes 'em any better than wot I am? They never did a day's work in their lives. I see 'em day after day——

MRS. JONES. And I wish you wouldn't come after me like that, and hang about the house. You don't seem able to keep away at all, and whatever you do it for I can't think, because of course they notice it.

JONES. I suppose I may go where I like. Where *may* I go? The other day I went to a place in the Edgeware Road. "Guv'nor," I says to the boss, "take me on," I says. "I 'aven't done a stroke o' work not these two months; it takes the heart out of a man," I says; "I'm one to work; I'm not afraid of anything you can give me!" "My good man," 'e says, "I've had thirty of you here this morning. I took the first two," he says, "and that's all I want." "Thank you, then rot the world!" I says. "Blasphemin'," he says, "is not the way to get a job. Out you go, my lad!" [*He laughs sardonically.*] Don't you raise your voice because you're starvin'; don't yer even think of it; take it lyin' down! Take it like a sensible man, carn't you? And a little way down the street a lady says to me: [*Pinching his voice.*] "D'you want to earn a few pence, my man?" and gives me her dog to 'old outside a shop—fat as a butler 'e was—tons o' meat had gone to the makin' of *him*. It did 'er good, it did, made 'er feel 'erself that *charitable*, but I see 'er lookin' at the copper standin' alongside o' me, for fear I should make off with 'er bloomin' fat dog. [*He sits on the edge of the bed and puts a boot on. Then looking up.*] What's in that head o' yours? [*Almost pathetically.*] Carn't you speak for once?

[*There is a knock, and* MRS. SEDDON, *the landlady, appears, an anxious, harassed, shabby woman in working clothes.*]

MRS. SEDDON. I thought I 'eard you come in, Mrs. Jones. I've spoke to my 'usband, but he says he really can't afford to wait another day.

JONES. [*With scowling jocularity*] Never you mind what your 'usband says, you go your own way like a proper independent woman. Here, Jenny, chuck her that.

[*Producing a sovereign from his trousers pocket, he throws it to his wife, who catches it in her apron with a gasp.* JONES *resumes the lacing of his boots.*]

MRS. JONES. [*Rubbing the sovereign stealthily*] I'm very

sorry we're so late with it, and of course it's fourteen shillings, so if you've got six that will be right.

[MRS. SEDDON *takes the sovereign and fumbles for the change.*

JONES. [*With his eyes fixed on his boots*] Bit of a surprise for yer, ain't it?

MRS. SEDDON.   Thank you, and I'm sure I'm very much obliged. [*She does indeed appear surprised.*]   I'll bring you the change.

JONES.   [*Mockingly*] Don't mention it.

MRS. SEDDON.   Thank you, and I'm sure I'm very much obliged.   [*She slides away.*

[MRS. JONES *gazes at* JONES, *who.is still lacing up his boots.*

JONES.   I've had a bit of luck. [*Pulling out the crimson purse and some loose coins.*]   Picked up a purse—seven pound and more.

MRS. JONES.   Oh, James!

JONES.   Oh, James!   What about Oh, James!   I picked it up I tell you.   This is lost property, this is!

MRS. JONES.   But isn't there a name in it, or something?

JONES.   Name?   No, there ain't no name.   This don't belong to such as 'ave visitin' cards.   This belongs to a perfec' lidy.   Tike an' smell it. [*He pitches her the purse, which she puts gently to her nose.*]   Now, you tell me what I ought to have done.   You tell me that.   You can always tell me what I ought to ha' done, can't yer?

MRS. JONES.   [*Laying down the purse*] I can't say what you ought to have done, James.   Of course the money wasn't yours; you've taken somebody else's money.

JONES.   Finding's keeping.   I'll take it as wages for the time I've gone about the streets asking for what's my rights. I'll take it for what's *overdue*, d'ye hear?   [*With strange triumph.*]   I've got money in my pocket, my girl.   [MRS. JONES *goes on again with the preparation of the meal*, JONES *looking at her furtively.*]   Money in my pocket!   And I'm not goin' to waste it.   With this 'ere money I'm goin' to Canada. I'll let you have a pound.   [*A silence.*]   You've often talked of leavin' me. You've often told me I treat you badly—well, I 'ope you'll be glad when I'm gone.

Mrs. Jones. [*Impassively*] You *have* treated me very badly, James, and of course I can't prevent your going; but I can't tell whether I shall be glad when you're gone.

Jones. It'll change my luck. I've 'ad nothing but bad luck since I first took up with you. [*More softly.*] And you've 'ad no bloomin' picnic.

Mrs. Jones. Of course it would have been better for us if we had never met. We weren't meant for each other. But you're set against me, that's what you are, and you *have* been for a long time. And you treat me so badly, James, going after that Rosie and all. You don't ever seem to think of the children that I've had to bring into the world, and of all the trouble I've had to keep them, and what'll become of them when you're gone.

Jones. [*Crossing the room gloomily*] If you think I want to leave the little beggars you're bloomin' well mistaken.

Mrs. Jones. Of course I know you're fond of them.

Jones. [*Fingering the purse, half angrily*] Well, then, you stow it, old girl. The kids'll get along better with you than when I'm here. If I'd ha' known as much as I do now, I'd never ha' had one o' them. What's the use o' bringin' 'em into a state o' things like this? It's a crime, that's what it is; but you find it out too late; that's what's the matter with this 'ere world. [*He puts the purse back in his pocket.*

Mrs. Jones. Of course it would have been better for them, poor little things; but they're your own children, and I wonder at you talkin' like that. I should miss them dreadfully if I was to lose them.

Jones. [*Sullenly*] An' you ain't the only one. If I make money out there—— [*Looking up, he sees her shaking out his coat—in a changed voice*] Leave that coat alone!

[*The silver box drops from the pocket, scattering the cigarettes upon the bed. Taking up the box, she stares at it; he rushes at her and snatches the box away.*

MRS. JONES. [*Cowering back against the bed*] Oh, Jem!
oh, Jem!

JONES. [*Dropping the box on to the table*] You mind what
you're sayin'! When I go out I'll take and chuck it in the
water along with that there purse. I 'ad it when I was in
liquor, and for what you do when you're in liquor you're not
responsible—and that's Gawd's truth as you ought to know. I
don't want the thing—I won't have it. I took it out o' spite.
I'm no thief, I tell you; and don't you call me one, or it'll be
the worse for you.

MRS. JONES. [*Twisting her apron strings*] It's Mr. Barthwick's! You've taken away my reputation. Oh, Jem,
whatever made you?

JONES. What d'you mean?

MRS. JONES. It's been missed; they think it's me. Oh!
whatever made you do it, Jem?

JONES. I tell you I was in liquor. I don't want it; what's
the good of it to me? If I were to pawn it they'd only nab me.
I'm no thief. I'm no worse than wot that young Barthwick
is; he brought 'ome that purse that I picked up—a lady's
purse—'ad it off 'er in a row, kept sayin' 'e'd scored 'er off.
Well, I scored 'im off. Tight as an owl 'e was! And d'you
think anything'll happen to him?

MRS. JONES. [*As though speaking to herself*] Oh, Jem! it's
the bread out of our mouths!

JONES. Is it then? I'll make it hot for 'em yet. What
about that purse? What about young Barthwick? [MRS.
JONES *comes forward to the table and tries to take the box;*
JONES *prevents her.*] What do you want with that? You
drop it, I say!

MRS. JONES. I'll take it back and tell them all about it.

[*She attempts to wrest the box from him.*

JONES. Ah, would yer?

[*He drops the box, and rushes on her with a snarl. She slips
back past the bed. He follows; a chair is overturned. The door
is opened;* SNOW *comes in, a detective in plain clothes and bowler*

hat, with clipped moustaches. JONES *drops his arms,* MRS. JONES *stands by the window gasping;* SNOW, *advancing swiftly to the table, puts his hand on the silver box.*

SNOW. Doin' a bit o' skylarkin'? Fancy this is what I'm after. J.B., the very same. [*He gets back to the door, scrutinizing the crest and cypher on the box. To* MRS. JONES.] I'm a police officer. Are you Mrs. Jones.

MRS. JONES. Yes, sir.

SNOW. My instructions are to take you on a charge of stealing this box from J. Barthwick, Esquire, M.P., of 6, Rockingham Gate. Anything you say may be used against you. Well, Missis?

MRS. JONES. [*In her quiet voice, still out of breath, her hand upon her breast*] Of course I did *not* take it, sir. I never have taken anything that didn't belong to me; and of course I know nothing about it.

SNOW. You were at the house this morning; you did the room in which the box was left; you were alone in the room. I find the box 'ere. You say you didn't take it?

MRS. JONES. Yes, sir, of course I say I did not take it, because I did *not*.

SNOW. Then how does the box come to be here?

MRS. JONES. I would rather not say anything about it.

SNOW. Is this your husband?

MRS. JONES. Yes, sir, this is my husband, sir.

SNOW. Do you wish to say anything before I take her? [JONES *remains silent, with his head bent down.*] Well then, Missis, I'll just trouble you to come along with me quietly.

MRS. JONES. [*Twisting her hands*] Of course I wouldn't say I hadn't taken it if I had—and I *didn't* take it, indeed I didn't. Of course I know appearances are against me, and I can't tell you what really happened. But my children are at school, and they'll be coming home—and I don't know what they'll do without me!

SNOW. Your 'usband'll see to them, don't you worry.
[*He takes the woman gently by the arm.*

JONES.   You drop it—she's all right!   [*Sullenly.*]   I took the thing myself.

SNOW.   [*Eyeing him*] There, there, it does you credit.   Come along, Missis.

JONES.   [*Passionately*] Drop it, I say, you blooming teck. She's my wife; she's a respectable woman.   Take her if you dare!

SNOW.   Now, now.   What's the good of this?   Keep a civil tongue, and it'll be the better for all of us.   [*He puts his whistle in his mouth and draws the woman to the door.*

JONES.   [*With a rush*] Drop her, and put up your 'ands, or I'll soon make yer.   You leave her alone, will yer!   Don't I tell yer, I took the thing myself!

SNOW.   [*Blowing his whistle*] Drop your hands, or I'll take you too.   Ah, would you?

[JONES, *closing, deals him a blow.   A Policeman in uniform appears; there is a short struggle, and* JONES *is overpowered.* MRS. JONES *raises her hands and drops her face on them.*

The curtain falls.

SCENE II

The BARTHWICKS' *dining-room the same evening.   The* BARTH-WICKS *are seated at dessert.*

MRS. BARTHWICK.   John!   [*A silence broken by the cracking of nuts.*]   John!

BARTHWICK.   I wish you'd speak about the nuts—they're uneatable.   [*He puts one in his mouth.*

MRS. BARTHWICK.   It's not the season for them.   I called on the Holyroods.   [BARTHWICK *fills his glass with port.*

JACK.   Crackers, please, dad.

[BARTHWICK *passes the crackers.   His demeanour is reflective.*

MRS. BARTHWICK.   Lady Holyrood has got very stout. I've noticed it coming for a long time.

BARTHWICK. [*Gloomily*] Stout? [*He takes up the crackers —with transparent airiness.*] The Holyroods had some trouble with their servants, hadn't they?

JACK. Crackers, please, dad.

BARTHWICK. [*Passing the crackers*] It got into the papers. The cook, wasn't it?

MRS. BARTHWICK. No, the lady's-maid. I was talking it over with Lady Holyrood. The girl used to have her young man to see her.

BARTHWICK. [*Uneasily*] I'm not sure they were wise——

MRS. BARTHWICK. My dear John, what are you talking about? How could there be any alternative? Think of the effect on the other servants!

BARTHWICK. Of course in principle—I wasn't thinking of that.

JACK. [*Maliciously*] Crackers, please, dad.

[BARTHWICK *is compelled to pass the crackers.*

MRS. BARTHWICK. Lady Holyrood told me: "I had her up," she said; "I said to her, 'You'll leave my house at once; I think your conduct disgraceful. I can't tell, I don't know, and I don't wish to know, what you were doing. I send you away on principle; you need not come to me for a character.' And the girl said: 'If you don't give me my notice, my lady, I want a month's wages. I'm perfectly respectable. I've done nothing.'"—Done nothing!

BARTHWICK. H'm!

MRS. BARTHWICK. Servants have too much licence. They hang together so terribly you never can tell what they're really thinking; it's as if they were all in a conspiracy to keep you in the dark. Even with Marlow, you feel that he never lets you know what's really in his mind. I hate that secretiveness; it destroys all confidence. I feel sometimes I should like to shake him.

JACK. Marlow's a most decent chap. It's simply beastly every one knowing your affairs.

BARTHWICK. The less you say about that the better!

MRS. BARTHWICK. It goes all through the lower classes. You can *not* tell when they are speaking the truth. To-day when I was shopping after leaving the Holyroods, one of these unemployed came up and spoke to me. I suppose I only had twenty yards or so to walk to the carriage, but he seemed to spring up in the street.

BARTHWICK. Ah! You must be very careful whom you speak to in these days.

MRS. BARTHWICK. I didn't answer him, of course. But I could see at once that he wasn't telling the truth.

BARTHWICK. [*Cracking a nut*] There's one very good rule —look at their eyes.

JACK. Crackers, please, dad.

BARTHWICK. [*Passing the crackers*] If their eyes are straight-forward I sometimes give them sixpence. It's against my principles, but it's most difficult to refuse. If you see that they're desperate, and dull, and shifty-looking, as so many of them are, it's certain to mean drink, or crime, or something unsatisfactory.

MRS. BARTHWICK. This man had dreadful eyes. He looked as if he could commit a murder. "I've 'ad nothing to eat to-day," he said. Just like that.

BARTHWICK. What was William about? He ought to have been waiting.

JACK. [*Raising his wineglass to his nose*] Is this the '63, dad?

[BARTHWICK, *holding his wineglass to his eye, lowers it and passes it before his nose.*

MRS. BARTHWICK. I hate people that can't speak the truth. [*Father and son exchange a look behind their port.*] It's just as easy to speak the truth as not. *I've* always found it easy enough. It makes it impossible to tell what is genuine; one feels as if one were continually being taken in.

BARTHWICK. [*Sententiously*] The lower classes are their own enemies. If they would only trust us, they would get on so much better.

MRS. BARTHWICK. But even then it's so often their own fault. Look at that Mrs. Jones this morning.

BARTHWICK. I only want to do what's right in that matter. I had occasion to see Roper this afternoon. I mentioned it to him. He's coming in this evening. It all depends on what the detective says. I've had my doubts. I've been thinking it over.

MRS. BARTHWICK. The woman impressed me most unfavourably. She seemed to have no shame. That affair she was talking about—she and the man when they were young, so immoral! And before you and Jack! I could have put her out of the room!

BARTHWICK. Oh! I don't want to excuse them, but in looking at these matters one must consider——

MRS. BARTHWICK. Perhaps you'll say the man's employer was wrong in dismissing him?

BARTHWICK. Of course not. It's not there that I feel doubt. What I ask myself is——

JACK. Port, please, dad.

BARTHWICK. [*Circulating the decanter in religious imitation of the rising and setting of the sun*] I ask myself whether we are sufficiently careful in making inquiries about people before we engage them, especially as regards moral conduct.

JACK. Pass the port, please, mother!

MRS. BARTHWICK. [*Passing it*] My dear boy, aren't you drinking too much? [JACK *fills his glass.*

MARLOW. [*Entering*] Detective Snow to see you, sir.

BARTHWICK. [*Uneasily*] Ah! say I'll be with him in a minute.

MRS. BARTHWICK. [*Without turning*] Let him come in here, Marlow.

[SNOW *enters in an overcoat, his bowler hat in hand.*

BARTHWICK. [*Half rising*] Oh! Good evening!

SNOW. Good evening, sir; good evening, ma'am. I've called round to report what I've done, rather late, I'm afraid—another case took me away. [*He takes the silver box out of his*

pocket, causing a sensation in the BARTHWICK *family.*]   This is
the identical article, I believe.

BARTHWICK.   Certainly, certainly.

SNOW.   Havin' your crest and cypher, as you described to
me, sir, I'd no hesitation in the matter.

BARTHWICK.   Excellent.   Will you have a glass of—[*he
glances at the waning port*]—er—sherry?   [*Pours out sherry.*]
Jack, just give Mr. Snow this.

[JACK *rises and gives the glass to* SNOW; *then, lolling in his
chair, regards him indolently.*

SNOW.   [*Drinking off wine and putting down the glass*] After
seeing you I went round to this woman's lodgings, sir.   It's a
low neighbourhood, and I thought it as well to place a constable
below—and not without 'e was wanted, as things turned out.

BARTHWICK.   Indeed!

SNOW.   Yes, sir, I 'ad some trouble.   I asked her to account
for the presence of the article.   She could give me no answer,
except to deny the theft; so I took her into custody; then her
husband came for me, so I was obliged to take him, too, for
assault.   He was very violent on the way to the station—very
violent—threatened you and your son, and altogether he was a
handful, I can tell you.

MRS. BARTHWICK.   What a ruffian he must be!

SNOW.   Yes, ma'am, a rough customer.

JACK.   [*Sipping his wine, bemused*] Punch the beggar's head.

SNOW.   Given to drink, as I understand, sir.

MRS. BARTHWICK.   It's to be hoped he will get a severe
punishment.

SNOW.   The odd thing is, sir, that he persists in sayin' he
took the box himself.

BARTHWICK.   Took the box himself!   [*He smiles.*]   What
does he think to gain by that?

SNOW.   He says the young gentleman was intoxicated last
night—[JACK *stops the cracking of a nut, and looks at* SNOW.
BARTHWICK, *losing his smile, has put his wineglass down; there
is a silence—*SNOW, *looking from face to face, remarks*]—took him

into the house and gave him whisky; and under the influence of an empty stomach the man says he took the box.

MRS. BARTHWICK.   The impudent wretch!

BARTHWICK.   D'you mean that he—er—intends to put this forward to-morrow——

SNOW.   That'll be his line, sir; but whether he's endeavouring to shield his wife, or whether [*he looks at* JACK] there's something in it, will be for the magistrate to say.

MRS. BARTHWICK.   [*Haughtily*] Something in what? I don't understand you.   As if my son would bring a man like that into the house!

BARTHWICK.   [*From the fireplace, with an effort to be calm*] My son can speak for himself, no doubt.—Well, Jack, what do you say?

MRS. BARTHWICK.   [*Sharply*] What does he say?   Why, of course, he says the whole story's stuff!

JACK.   [*Embarrassed*] Well, of course, I—of course, I don't know anything about it.

MRS. BARTHWICK.   I should think not, indeed! [*To* SNOW.]   The man is an audacious ruffian!

BARTHWICK.   [*Suppressing jumps*] But in view of my son's saying there's nothing in this—this fable—will it be necessary to proceed against the man under the circumstances?

SNOW.   We shall have to charge him with the assault, sir. It would be as well for your son to come down to the Court. There'll be a remand, no doubt.   The queer thing is there was quite a sum of money found on him, and a crimson silk purse. [BARTHWICK *starts;* JACK *rises and sits down again.*] I suppose the lady hasn't missed her purse?

BARTHWICK.   [*Hastily*] Oh, no! Oh, no!

JACK.   No!

MRS. BARTHWICK.   [*Dreamily*] No! [*To* SNOW.]   I've been inquiring of the servants.   This man *does* hang about the house.   I shall feel much safer if he gets a good long sentence; I do think we ought to be protected against such ruffians.

BARTHWICK.   Yes, yes, of course, on principle—but in this

case we have a number of things to think of. [*To* Snow.]   I
suppose, as you say, the man *must* be charged, eh?

Snow.   No question about that, sir.

Barthwick.   [*Staring gloomily at* Jack] This prosecution
goes very much against the grain with me.   I have great
sympathy with the poor.   In my position I'm bound to recognize
the distress there is amongst them.   The condition of the people
leaves much to be desired.   D'you follow me?   I wish I could
see my way to drop it.

.Mrs. Barthwick.   [*Sharply*] John! it's simply not fair
to other people.   It's putting property at the mercy of anyone
who likes to take it.

Barthwick.   [*Trying to make signs to her aside*] I'm not
defending him, not at all.   I'm trying to look at the matter
broadly.

Mrs. Barthwick.   Nonsense, John, there's a time for
everything.

Snow.   [*Rather sardonically*] I might point out, sir, that to
withdraw the charge of stealing would not make much difference, because the facts must come out [*he looks significantly at*
Jack] in reference to the assault; and, as I said, that charge will
have to go forward.

Barthwick.   [*Hastily*] Yes, oh! exactly!   It's entirely on
the woman's account—entirely a matter of my own private
feelings.

Snow.   If I were you, sir, I should let things take their
course.   It's not likely there'll be much difficulty.   These
things are very quick settled.

Barthwick.   [*Doubtfully*] You think so—you think so?

Jack.   [*Rousing himself*] I say, what shall I have to swear
to?

Snow.   That's best known to yourself, sir.   [*Retreating to
the door.*]   Better employ a solicitor, sir, in case anything should
arise.   We shall have the butler to prove the loss of the article.
You'll excuse me going, I'm rather pressed to-night.   The case
may come on any time after eleven.   Good evening, sir; good

evening, ma'am. I shall have to produce the box in court to-morrow, so if you'll excuse me, sir, I may as well take it with me.

[*He takes the silver box and leaves them with a little bow.*

[BARTHWICK *makes a move to follow him, then dashing his hands beneath his coat tails, speaks with desperation.*

BARTHWICK. I do wish you'd leave me to manage things myself. You *will* put your nose into matters you know nothing of. A pretty mess you've made of this!

MRS. BARTHWICK. [*Coldly*] I don't in the least know what you're talking about. If you can't stand up for your rights, I can. I've no patience with your principles, it's such nonsense.

BARTHWICK. Principles! Good Heavens! What have principles to do with it, for goodness' sake? Don't you know that Jack was drunk last night!

JACK. Dad!

MRS. BARTHWICK. [*In horror rising*] Jack!

JACK. Look here, mother—I had supper. Everybody does. I mean to say—you know what I mean—it's absurd to call it being drunk. At Oxford everybody gets a bit "on" sometimes——

MRS. BARTHWICK. Well I think it's most dreadful! If that is really what you do at Oxford——

JACK. [*Angrily*] Well, why did you send me there? One must do as other fellows do. It's such nonsense, I mean, to call it being drunk. Of course I'm awfully sorry. I've had such a beastly headache all day.

BARTHWICK. Tcha! If you'd only had the common decency to remember what happened when you came in. Then we should know what truth there was in what this fellow says —as it is, it's all the most confounded darkness.

JACK. [*Staring as though at half-formed visions*] I just get a—and then—it's gone——

MRS. BARTHWICK. Oh, Jack! do you mean to say you were so tipsy you can't even remember——

JACK. Look here, mother! Of course I remember I came —I must have come——

BARTHWICK. [*Unguardedly, and walking up and down*] Tcha!—and that infernal purse! Good Heavens! It'll get into the papers. Who on earth could have foreseen a thing like this? Better to have lost a dozen cigarette-boxes, and said nothing about it. [*To his wife.*] It's all your doing. I told you so from the first. I wish to goodness Roper would come!

MRS. BARTHWICK. [*Sharply*] I don't know what you're talking about, John.

BARTHWICK. [*Turning on her*] No, you—you—you don't know anything! [*Sharply.*] Where the devil is Roper? If he can see a way out of this he's a better man than I take him for. I defy *anyone* to see a way out of it. *I* can't.

JACK. Look here, don't excite, dad—I can simply say I was too beastly tired, and don't remember anything except that I came in and [*in a dying voice*] went to bed the same as usual.

BARTHWICK. Went to bed? Who knows where you went?—I've lost all confidence. For all I know you slept on the floor.

JACK. [*Indignantly*] I didn't, I slept on the——

BARTHWICK. [*Sitting on the sofa*] Who cares where you slept; what does it matter if he mentions the—the—a perfect disgrace?

MRS. BARTHWICK. *What?* [*A silence.*] I *insist* on knowing.

JACK. Oh! nothing——

MRS. BARTHWICK. Nothing? What do you mean by nothing, Jack? There's your father in such a state about it——

JACK. It's only my purse.

MRS. BARTHWICK. Your purse. You know perfectly well you haven't got one.

JACK. Well, it was somebody else's—It was all a joke—I didn't want the beastly thing——

MRS. BARTHWICK. Do you mean that you had another person's purse, and that this man took it too?

BARTHWICK. Tcha! Of course he took it too! A man

like that Jones will make the most of it. It'll get into the papers.

MRS. BARTHWICK. I don't understand. What on earth is all the fuss about? [*Bending over* JACK, *and softly.*] Jack, now tell me, dear! Don't be afraid. What is it? Come!

JACK. Oh, don't, mother!

MRS. BARTHWICK. But don't what, dear?

JACK. It was pure sport. I don't know how I got the thing. Of course I'd had a bit of a row—I didn't know what I was doing—I was—I was—well, you know—I suppose I must have pulled the bag out of her hand.

MRS. BARTHWICK. Out of her hand? Whose hand? What bag—whose bag?

JACK. Oh! I don't know—*her* bag—it belonged to—[*in a desperate and rising voice*] a woman.

MRS. BARTHWICK. A woman? *Oh! Jack! No!*

JACK. [*Jumping up*] You *would* have it. I didn't want to tell you. It's not my fault.

[*The door opens and* MARLOW *ushers in a man of middle age, inclined to corpulence, in evening dress. He has a ruddy, thin moustache, and dark, quick-moving little eyes. His eyebrows are Chinese.*

MARLOW. Mr. Roper, sir. [*He leaves the room.*

ROPER. [*With a quick look round*] How do you do?

[*But neither* JACK *nor* MRS. BARTHWICK *make a sign.*

BARTHWICK. [*Hurrying*] Thank goodness you've come, Roper. You remember what I told you this afternoon; we've just had the detective here.

ROPER. Got the box?

BARTHWICK. Yes, yes, but look here—it wasn't the char-woman at all; her drunken loafer of a husband took the things—he says that fellow there [*he waves his hand at* JACK, *who with his shoulder raised, seems trying to ward off a blow*] let him into the house last night. Can you imagine such a thing?

[*Roper laughs.*

BARTHWICK. [*With excited emphasis*] It's no laughing

matter, Roper. I told you about that business of Jack's too—don't you see—the brute took both the things—took that infernal purse. It'll get into the papers.

ROPER. [*Raising his eyebrows*] H'm! The purse! Depravity in high life! What does your son say?

BARTHWICK. He remembers nothing. D——n! Did you ever see such a mess? It'll get into the papers.

MRS. BARTHWICK. [*With her hand across her eyes*] No! it's not that—— [BARTHWICK *and* ROPER *turn and look at her*.

BARTHWICK. It's the idea of that woman—she's just heard—— [ROPER *nods. And* MRS. BARTHWICK, *setting her lips, gives a slow look at* JACK, *and sits down at the table*]. What on earth's to be done, Roper? A ruffian like this Jones will make all the capital he can out of that purse.

MRS. BARTHWICK. I don't believe that Jack took that purse.

BARTHWICK. What—when the woman came here for it this morning?

MRS. BARTHWICK. Here? She had the impudence? Why wasn't I told? [*She looks round from face to face—no one answers her, there is a pause.*

BARTHWICK. [*Suddenly*] What's to be done, Roper?

ROPER. [*Quietly to* JACK] I suppose you didn't leave your latchkey in the door?

JACK. [*Sullenly*] Yes, I did.

BARTHWICK. Good heavens! What next?

MRS. BARTHWICK. I'm certain you never let that man into the house, Jack, it's a wild invention. I'm sure there's not a word of truth in it, Mr. Roper.

ROPER. [*Very suddenly*] Where did you sleep last night?

JACK. [*Promptly*] On the sofa, there—[*hesitating*] that is—I——

BARTHWICK. On the sofa? D'you mean to say you didn't go to bed?

JACK. [*Sullenly*] No.

BARTHWICK. If you don't remember anything, how can you remember that?

JACK. Because I woke up there in the morning.

MRS. BARTHWICK. Oh, Jack!

BARTHWICK. Good gracious!

JACK. And Mrs. Jones saw me. I wish you wouldn't bait me so.

ROPER. Do you remember giving anyone a drink?

JACK. By Jove, I do seem to remember a fellow with—a fellow with—— [*He looks at Roper*] I say, d'you want me——?

ROPER. [*Quick as lightning*] With a dirty face?

JACK. [*With illumination*] I do—I distinctly remember his——

[BARTHWICK *moves abruptly;* MRS. BARTHWICK *looks at* ROPER *angrily, and touches her son's arm.*

MRS. BARTHWICK. You don't remember, it's ridiculous! I don't believe the man was ever here at all.

BARTHWICK. You must speak the truth, if it *is* the truth. But if you *do* remember such a dirty business, I shall wash my hands of you altogether.

JACK. [*Glaring at them*] Well, what the devil——

MRS. BARTHWICK. Jack!

JACK. Well, mother, I—I don't know what you *do* want.

MRS. BARTHWICK. We want you to speak the truth and say you never let this low man into the house.

BARTHWICK. Of course if you think that you really gave this man whisky in that disgraceful way, and let him see what you'd been doing, and were in such a disgusting condition that you don't remember a word of it——

ROPER. [*Quick*] I've no memory myself—never had.

BARTHWICK. [*Desperately*] I don't know what you're to say.

ROPER. [*To* JACK] Say nothing at all! Don't put yourself in a false position. The man stole the things or the woman stole the things, you had nothing to do with it. You were asleep on the sofa.

MRS. BARTHWICK. Your leaving the latchkey in the door was quite bad enough, there's no need to mention anything else. [*Touching his forehead softly.*]   My dear, how hot your head is!

JACK.   But I want to know what I'm to do.   [*Passionately.*] I won't be badgered like this.

[MRS. BARTHWICK *recoils from him.*

ROPER.   [*Very quickly*] You forgot all about it.   You were asleep.

JACK.   Must I go down to the Court to-morrow?

ROPER.   [*Shaking his head*] No.

BARTHWICK.   [*In a relieved voice*] Is that so?

ROPER.   Yes.

BARTHWICK.   But *you'll* go, Roper.

ROPER.   Yes.

JACK.   [*With wan cheerfulness*] Thanks, awfully!   So long as I don't have to go.   [*Putting his hand up to his head.*]   I think if you'll excuse me—I've had a most beastly day.

[*He looks from his father to his mother.*

MRS. BARTHWICK.   [*Turning quickly*] Good night, my boy.

JACK.   Good-night, mother. [*He goes out.* MRS. BARTH-WICK *heaves a sigh.   There is a silence.*

BARTHWICK.   He gets off too easily.   But for my money that woman would have prosecuted him.

ROPER.   You find money useful.

BARTHWICK.   I've my doubts whether we ought to hide the truth——

ROPER.   There'll be a remand.

BARTHWICK.   What!   D'you mean he'll have to *appear* on the remand?

ROPER.   Yes.

BARTHWICK.   H'm, I thought you'd be able to——   Look here, Roper, you *must* keep that purse out of the papers.

[ROPER *fixes his little eyes on him and nods.*

MRS. BARTHWICK.   Mr. Roper, don't you think the magistrate ought to be told what sort of people these Joneses are; I mean about their immorality before they were married.   I don't know if John told you.

ROPER.   Afraid it's not material.

MRS. BARTHWICK.   Not material?

ROPER.   Purely private life!   May have happened to the magistrate.

BARTHWICK.   [*With a movement as if to shift a burden*] Then you'll take the thing into your hands?

ROPER.   If the gods are kind.   [*He holds his hand out.*

BARTHWICK.   [*Shaking it dubiously*] Kind—eh?   What? You going?

ROPER.   Yes.   I've another case, something like yours—most unexpected.

[*He bows to* MRS. BARTHWICK *and goes out, followed by* BARTHWICK, *talking to the last.* MRS. BARTHWICK *at the table bursts into smothered sobs.* BARTHWICK *returns.*

BARTHWICK.   [*To himself*] There'll be a scandal.

MRS. BARTHWICK.   [*Disguising her grief at once*] I simply can't imagine what Roper means by making a joke of a thing like that!

BARTHWICK.   [*Staring strangely*] You!   You can't imagine anything!   You've no more imagination than a fly!

MRS. BARTHWICK.   [*Angrily*] You dare to tell me that I have no imagination.

BARTHWICK.   [*Flustered*] I—I'm upset.   From beginning to end, the whole thing has been utterly against my principles.

MRS. BARTHWICK.   Rubbish!   You haven't any!   Your principles are nothing in the world but sheer—fright!

BARTHWICK.   [*Walking to the window*] I've never been frightened in my life.   You heard what Roper said.   It's enough to upset anyone when a thing like this happens.   Everything one says and does seems to turn in one's mouth—it's—it's uncanny.   It's not the sort of thing I've been accustomed to.   [*As though stifling, he throws the window open.   The faint sobbing of a child comes in.*]   What's that?   [*They listen.*

MRS. BARTHWICK.   [*Sharply*] I can't stand that crying.   I must send Marlow to stop it.   My nerves are all on edge. [*She rings the bell.*]

BARTHWICK.   I'll shut the window; you'll hear nothing.
[*He shuts the window.   There is silence.*]

MRS. BARTHWICK.   [*Sharply*] That's no good!   It's on my
nerves.   Nothing upsets me like a child's crying.   [MARLOW
comes in.]   What's that noise of crying, Marlow?   It sounds
like a child.

BARTHWICK.   It is a child.   I can see it against the railings.

MARLOW.   [*Opening the window, and looking out—quietly*]
It's Mrs. Jones's little boy, ma'am; he came here after his
mother.

MRS. BARTHWICK.   [*Moving quickly to the window*] Poor
little chap!   John, we oughtn't to go on with this!

BARTHWICK.   [*Sitting heavily in a chair*] Ah! but it's out
of our hands!

[MRS BARTHWICK *turns her back to the window.   There is
an expression of distress on her face.   She stands motionless, com-
pressing her lips.   The crying begins again.*   BARTHWICK *covers
his ears with his hands, and* MARLOW *shuts the window.   The
crying ceases.*

The curtain falls.

ACT III

Eight days have passed, and the scene is a London Police Court at one o'clock. A canopied seat of Justice is surmounted by the lion and unicorn. Before the fire a worn-looking MAGISTRATE *is warming his coat-tails, and staring at two little girls in faded blue and orange rags, who are placed before the dock. Close to the witness-box is a* RELIEVING OFFICER *in an overcoat, and a short brown beard. Beside the little girl stands a bald* POLICE CONSTABLE. *On the front bench are sitting* BARTHWICK *and* ROPER, *and behind them* JACK. *In the railed enclosure are seedy-looking men and women. Some prosperous constables sit or stand about.*

MAGISTRATE. [*In his paternal and ferocious voice, hissing his s's*] Now let us dispose of these young ladies.

USHER. Theresa Livens, Maud Livens. [*The bald* CONSTABLE *indicates the little girls, who remain silent, disillusioned, inattentive.*] Relieving Officer! [*The* RELIEVING OFFICER *steps into the witness-box.*

USHER. The evidence you give to the Court shall be the truth, the whole truth, and nothing but the truth, so help you God! Kiss the book! [*The book is kissed.*

RELIEVING OFFICER. [*In a monotone, pausing slightly at each sentence end, that his evidence may be inscribed*] About ten o'clock this morning, your Worship, I found these two little girls in Blue Street, Pulham, crying outside a public-house. Asked where their home was, they said they had no home. Mother had gone away. Asked about their father. Their father had no work. Asked where they slept last night. At their aunt's. I've made inquiries, your Worship. The wife has broken up the home and gone on the streets. The husband is out of work

47

and living in common lodging-houses. The husband's sister has eight children of her own, and says she can't afford to keep these little girls any longer.

MAGISTRATE. [*Returning to his seat beneath the canopy of Justice*] Now, let me see. You say the mother is on the streets; what evidence have you of that?

RELIEVING OFFICER. I have the husband here, your Worship.

MAGISTRATE. Very well; then let us see him. [*There are cries of* "LIVENS." *The* MAGISTRATE *leans forward, and stares with hard compassion at the little girls.* LIVENS *comes in. He is quiet, with grizzled hair, and a muffler for a collar. He stands beside the witness-box.*] And you are their father? Now, why don't you keep your little girls at home? How is it you leave them to wander about the streets like this?

LIVENS. I've got no home, your Worship. I'm living from 'and to mouth. I've got no work; and nothin' to keep them on.

MAGISTRATE. How is that?

LIVENS. [*Ashamedly*] My wife, she broke my 'ome up, and pawned the things.

MAGISTRATE. But what made you let her?

LIVENS. Your Worship, I'd no chance to stop 'er; she did it when I was out lookin' for work.

MAGISTRATE. Did you ill-treat her?

LIVENS. [*Emphatically*] I never raised my 'and to her in my life, your Worship.

MAGISTRATE. Then what was it—did she drink?

LIVENS. Yes, your Worship.

MAGISTRATE. Was she loose in her behaviour?

LIVENS. [*In a low voice*] Yes, your Worship.

MAGISTRATE. And where is she now?

LIVENS. I don't know, your Worship. She went off with a man, and after that I——

MAGISTRATE. Yes, yes. Who knows anything of her? [*To the bald* CONSTABLE] Is she known here?

RELIEVING OFFICER. Not in this district, your Worship; but I have ascertained that she is well known——

MAGISTRATE. Yes—yes; we'll stop at that. Now [*to the Father*] you say that she has broken up your home, and left these little girls. What provision can you make for them? You look a strong man.

LIVENS. So I am, your Worship. I'm willin' enough to work, but for the life of me I can't get anything to do.

MAGISTRATE. But have you tried?

LIVENS. I've tried everything, your Worship—I've tried my 'ardest.

MAGISTRATE. Well, well—— [*There is a silence.*

RELIEVING OFFICER. If your Worship thinks it's a case, my people are willing to take them.

MAGISTRATE. Yes, yes, I know; but I've no evidence that this man is not the proper guardian for his children.

[*He rises and goes back to the fire.*

RELIEVING OFFICER. The mother, your Worship, is able to get access to them.

MAGISTRATE. Yes, yes; the mother, of course, is an improper person to have anything to do with them. [*To the Father*] Well, now what do you say?

LIVENS. Your Worship, I can only say that if I could get work I should be only too willing to provide for them. But what can I do, your Worship? Here I am, obliged to live from 'and to mouth in these 'ere common lodging-houses. I'm a strong man—I'm willing to work—I'm half as alive again as some of 'em—but you see, your Worship, my 'air's turned a bit, owing to the fever—[*Touches his hair.*]—and that's against me; and I don't seem to get a chance anyhow.

MAGISTRATE. Yes—yes. [*Slowly.*] Well, I think it's a case. [*Staring his hardest at the little girls.*] Now are you willing that these little girls should be sent to a home?

LIVENS. Yes, your Worship, I should be very willing.

MAGISTRATE. Well, I'll remand them for a week. Bring

them again to-day week; if I see no reason against it then, I'll make an order.

RELIEVING OFFICER.   To-day week, your Worship.

[*The bald* CONSTABLE *takes the little girls out by the shoulders. The father follows them.   The* MAGISTRATE, *returning to his seat, bends over and talks to his* CLERK *inaudibly.*

BARTHWICK.   [*Speaking behind his hand*] A painful case, Roper; very distressing state of things.

ROPER.   Hundreds like this in the police courts.

BARTHWICK.   Most distressing!   The more I see of it, the more important this question of the condition of the people seems to become.   I shall certainly make a point of taking up the cudgels in the House.   I shall move——

[*The* MAGISTRATE *ceases talking to his* CLERK.

CLERK.   Remands.

[BARTHWICK *stops abruptly.   There is a stir and* MRS. JONES *comes in by the public door;* JONES, *ushered by policemen, comes from the prisoner's door.   They file into the dock.*

CLERK.   James Jones, Jane Jones.

USHER.   Jane Jones.

BARTHWICK.   [*In a whisper*] The purse—the purse *must* be kept out of it, Roper.   Whatever happens you must keep that out of the papers.   [ROPER *nods.*

BALD CONSTABLE.   Hush!

[MRS. JONES, *dressed in her thin, black, wispy dress, and black straw hat, stands motionless with hands crossed on the front rail of the dock.*   JONES *leans against the back rail of the dock, and keeps half turning, glancing defiantly about him.   He is haggard and unshaven.*

CLERK.   [*Consulting with his papers*] This is the case remanded from last Wednesday, sir.   Theft of a silver cigarette-box and assault on the police; the two charges were taken together.   Jane Jones!   James Jones!

MAGISTRATE.   [*Staring*] Yes, yes; I remember.

CLERK.   Jane Jones.

MRS. JONES.   Yes, sir.

CLERK. Do you admit stealing a silver cigarette-box valued at five pounds, ten shillings, from the house of John Barthwick, M.P., between the hours of 11 P.M. on Easter Monday and 8.45 A.M. on Easter Tuesday last? Yes or no?

MRS. JONES. [*In a low voice*] No, sir, I do not, sir.

CLERK. James Jones? Do you admit stealing a silver cigarette-box valued at five pounds, ten shillings, from the house of John Barthwick, M.P., between the hours of 11 P.M. on Easter Monday and 8.45 A.M. on Easter Tuesday last? And further making an assault on the police when in the execution of their duty at 3 P.M. on Easter Tuesday? Yes or no?

JONES. [*Sullenly*] Yes, but I've a lot to say about it.

MAGISTRATE. [*To the* CLERK] Yes—yes. But how comes it that these two people are charged with the same offence? Are they husband and wife?

CLERK. Yes, sir. You remember you ordered a remand for further evidence as to the story of the male prisoner.

MAGISTRATE. Have they been in custody since?

CLERK. You released the woman on her own recognizances, sir.

MAGISTRATE. Yes, yes, this is the case of the silver box; I remember now. Well?

CLERK. Thomas Marlow.

[*The cry of* "THOMAS MARLOW" *is repeated.* MARLOW *comes in, and steps into the witness-box, and is sworn. The silver box is handed up, and placed on the rail.*

CLERK. [*Reading from his papers*] Your name is Thomas Marlow? Are you butler to John Barthwick, M.P., of 6, Rockingham Gate?

MARLOW. Yes, sir.

CLERK. Did you between 10.45 and 11 o'clock on the night of Easter Monday last place a silver cigarette-box on a tray on the dining-room table at 6, Rockingham Gate? Is that the box?

MARLOW. Yes, sir.

CLERK.   And did you miss the same at 8.45 on the following morning, on going to remove the tray?

MARLOW.   Yes, sir.

CLERK.   Is the female prisoner known to you?

                                                    [MARLOW *nods.*

Is she the charwoman employed at 6, Rockingham Gate?

                                                    [*Again* MARLOW *nods.*

Did you at the time of your missing the box find her in the room alone?

MARLOW.   Yes, sir.

CLERK.   Did you afterwards communicate the loss to your employer, and did he send you to the police station?

MARLOW.   Yes, sir.

CLERK.   [*To* MRS. JONES] Have you anything to ask him?

MRS. JONES.   No, sir, nothing, thank you, sir.

CLERK.   [*To* JONES] James Jones, have you anything to ask this witness?

JONES.   I don't know 'im.

MAGISTRATE.   Are you sure you put the box in the place you say at the time you say?

MARLOW.   Yes, your Worship.

MAGISTRATE.   Very well; then now let us have the officer.

                        [MARLOW *leaves the box, and* SNOW *goes into it.*

USHER.   The evidence you give to the court shall be the truth, the whole truth, and nothing but the truth, so help you God.   [*The book is kissed.*

CLERK.   [*Reading from his papers*] Your name is Robert Snow?   You are a detective in the X. B. division of the Metropolitan police force?   According to instructions received, did you on Easter Tuesday last proceed to the prisoners' lodgings at 34, Merthyr Street, St. Soames'?   And did you on entering see the box produced, lying on the table?

SNOW.   Yes, sir.

CLERK.   Is that the box?

SNOW.   [*Fingering the box*] Yes, sir.

CLERK. And did you thereupon take possession of it, and charge the female prisoner with theft of the box from 6, Rockingham Gate? And did she deny the same?

SNOW. Yes, sir.

CLERK. Did you take her into custody?

SNOW. Yes, sir.

MAGISTRATE. What was her behaviour?

SNOW. Perfectly quiet, your Worship. She persisted in the denial. That's all.

MAGISTRATE. Do you know her?

SNOW. No, your Worship.

MAGISTRATE. Is she known here?

BALD CONSTABLE. No, your Worship, they're neither of them known, we've nothing against them at all.

CLERK. [*To* MRS. JONES] Have you anything to ask the officer?

MRS. JONES. No, sir, thank you, I've nothing to ask him.

MAGISTRATE. Very well then—go on.

CLERK. [*Reading from his papers*] And while you were taking the female prisoner did the male prisoner interpose, and endeavour to hinder you in the execution of your duty, and did he strike you a blow?

SNOW. Yes, sir.

CLERK. And did he say, "You let her go, I took the box myself?"

SNOW. He did.

CLERK. And did you blow your whistle and obtain the assistance of another constable, and take him into custody?

SNOW. I did.

CLERK. Was he violent on the way to the station, and did he use bad language, and did he several times repeat that he had taken the box himself? [SNOW *nods.*

Did you thereupon ask him in what manner he had stolen the box? And did you understand him to say that he had entered the house at the invitation of young Mr. Barthwick [BARTHWICK, *turning in his seat, frowns at* ROPER] after midnight on Easter Monday, and partaken of whisky, and that under the influence of the whisky he had taken the box?

SNOW.   I did, sir.

CLERK.   And was his demeanour throughout very violent?

SNOW.   It *was* very violent.

JONES.   [*Breaking in*] Violent—of course it was.   You put your 'ands on my wife when I kept tellin' you I took the thing myself.

MAGISTRATE.   [*Hissing, with protruded neck*] Now—you will have your chance of saying what you want to say presently. Have you anything to ask the officer?

JONES.   [*Sullenly*] No.

MAGISTRATE.   Very well then.   Now let us hear what the female prisoner has to say first.

MRS. JONES.   Well, your Worship, of course I can only say what I've said all along, that I didn't take the box.

MAGISTRATE.   Yes, but did you know that it was taken?

MRS. JONES.   No, your Worship.   And, of course, as to what my husband says, your Worship, I can't speak of my own knowledge.   Of course, I know that he came home very late on the Monday night.   It was past one o'clock when he came in, and he was not himself at all.

MAGISTRATE.   Had he been drinking?

MRS. JONES.   Yes, your Worship.

MAGISTRATE.   And was he drunk?

MRS. JONES.   Yes, your Worship, he was almost quite drunk.

MAGISTRATE.   And did he say anything to you?

MRS. JONES.   No, your Worship, only to call me names. And of course in the morning when I got up and went to work he was asleep.   And I don't know anything more about it until I came home again.   Except that Mr. Barthwick—that's my employer, your Worship—told me the box was missing.

MAGISTRATE.   Yes, yes.

MRS. JONES.   But of course when I was shaking out my husband's coat the cigarette-box fell out and all the cigarettes were scattered on the bed.

MAGISTRATE. You say all the cigarettes were scattered on the bed? [*To* SNOW] Did you see the cigarettes scattered on the bed?

SNOW. No, your Worship, I did not.

MAGISTRATE. You see he says he didn't see them.

JONES. Well, they were there for all that.

SNOW. I can't say, your Worship, that I had the opportunity of going round the room; I had all my work cut out with the male prisoner.

MAGISTRATE. [*To* MRS. JONES] Well, what more have you to say?

MRS. JONES. Of course when I saw the box, your Worship, I was dreadfully upset, and I couldn't think why he had done such a thing; when the officer came we were having words about it, because it is ruin to me, your Worship, in my profession, and I have three little children dependent on me.

MAGISTRATE. [*Protruding his neck*] Yes—yes—but what did he say to you?

MRS. JONES. I asked him whatever came over him to do such a thing—and he said it was the drink. He said that he had had too much to drink, and something came over him. And of course, your Worship, he had had very little to eat all day, and the drink does go to the head when you have not had enough to eat. Your Worship may not know, but it is the truth. And I would like to say that all through his married life I have never known him to do such a thing before, though we have passed through great hardships, and [*speaking with soft emphasis*] I am quite sure he would not have done it if he had been himself at the time.

MAGISTRATE. Yes, yes. But don't you know that that is no excuse?

MRS. JONES. Yes, your Worship. I know that it is no excuse.

[*The* MAGISTRATE *leans over and parleys with his* CLERK.

JACK. [*Leaning over from his seat behind*] I say, dad——

BARTHWICK. Tsst! [*Sheltering his mouth, he speaks to*

Roper.] Roper, you had better get up now and say that considering the circumstances and the poverty of the prisoners, we have no wish to proceed any further, and if the magistrate would deal with the case as one of disorder only on the part of——

Bald Constable. Hssshh! [Roper *shakes his head.*

Magistrate. Now, supposing what you say and what your husband says is true, what I have to consider is—how did he obtain access to this house, and were you in any way a party to his obtaining access? You are the charwoman employed at the house?

Mrs. Jones. Yes, your Worship, and of course if I had let him into the house it would have been very wrong of me; and I have never done such a thing in any of the houses where I have been employed.

Magistrate. Well—so you say. Now let us hear what story the male prisoner makes of it.

Jones. [*Who leans with his arms on the dock behind, speaks in a slow, sullen voice*] Wot I say is wot my wife says. I've never been 'ad up in a police court before, an' I can prove I took it when in liquor. I told her, an' she can tell you the same, that I was goin' to throw the thing into the water sooner than 'ave it on my mind.

Magistrate. But how did you get into the *house?*

Jones. I was passin'. I was goin' 'ome from the "Goat and Bells."

Magistrate. The "Goat and Bells,"—what is that? A public-house?

Jones. Yes, at the corner. It was Bank 'oliday, an' I'd 'ad a drop to drink. I see this young Mr. Barthwick tryin' to find the keyhole on the wrong side of the door.

Magistrate. Well?

Jones. [*Slowly and with many pauses*] Well—I 'elped 'im to find it—drunk as a lord 'e was. He goes on, an' comes back again, and says, I've got nothin' for you, 'e says, but come in an' 'ave a drink. So I went in just as you might 'ave done yourself. We 'ad a drink o' whisky just as you might have 'ad, 'nd young

Mr. Brathwick says to me, "Take a drink 'nd a smoke. Take anything you like," 'e says. And then he went to sleep on the sofa. I 'ad some more whisky—an' I 'ad a smoke—and I 'ad some more whisky—an' I carn't tell yer what 'appened after that.

MAGISTRATE. Do you mean to say you were so drunk that you can remember nothing?

JACK. [*Softly to his father*] I say, that's exactly what——

BARTHWICK. Tssh!

JONES. That's what I do mean.

MAGISTRATE. And yet you say you stole the box?

JONES. I never stole the box. I took it.

MAGISTRATE. [*Hissing, with protruded neck*] You did not steal it—you took it. Did it belong to you—what is that but stealing?

JONES. I took it.

MAGISTRATE. You took it—you took it away from their house and you took it to your house——

JONES. [*Sullenly breaking in*] I ain't got a house.

MAGISTRATE. Very well, let us hear what this young man Mr.—Mr. Barthwick—has to say to your story.

[SNOW *leaves the witness-box. The* BALD CONSTABLE *beckons* JACK, *who, clutching his hat, goes into the witness-box.* ROPER *moves to the table set apart for his profession.*

SWEARING CLERK. The evidence you give to the Court shall be the truth, the whole truth, and nothing but the truth, so help you God. Kiss the book. [*The book is kissed.*

ROPER. [*Examining*] What is your name?

JACK. [*In a low voice*] John Barthwick, Junior.

[*The* CLERK *writes it down.*

ROPER. Where do you live?

JACK. At 6, Rockingham Gate.

[*All his answers are recorded by the* CLERK.

ROPER. You are the son of the owner?

JACK. [*In a very low voice*] Yes.

ROPER. Speak up, please. Do you know the prisoners?

JACK. [*Looking at the* JONESES, *in a low voice*] I've seen Mrs. Jones.   I—[*in a loud voice*] don't know the man.

JONES.   Well, I know you!

BALD CONSTABLE.   Hssh!

ROPER.   Now, did you come in late on the night of Easter Monday?

JACK.   Yes.

ROPER.   And did you by mistake leave your latchkey in the door?

JACK.   Yes.

MAGISTRATE.   Oh!   You left your latchkey in the door?

ROPER.   And is that all you can remember about your coming in?

JACK.   [*In a loud voice*] Yes, it is.

MAGISTRATE.   Now, you have heard the male prisoner's story, what do you say to that?

JACK.   [*Turning to the* MAGISTRATE, *speaks suddenly in a confident, straightforward voice*] The fact of the matter is, sir, that I'd been out to the theatre that night, and had supper afterwards, and I came in late.

MAGISTRATE.   Do you remember this man being outside when you came in?

JACK.   No, sir.   [*He hesitates.*]   I don't think I do.

MAGISTRATE.   [*Somewhat puzzled*] Well, did he help you to open the door, as he says?   Did *any*one help you to open the door?

JACK.   No, sir—I don't think so, sir—I don't know.

MAGISTRATE.   You don't know?   But you must know.   It isn't a usual thing for you to have the door opened for you, is it?

JACK.   [*With a shameful smile*] No.

MAGISTRATE.   Very well, then——

JACK.   [*Desperately*] The fact of the matter is, sir, I'm afraid I'd had too much champagne that night.

MAGISTRATE.   [*Smiling*] Oh!   you'd had too much champagne?

JONES.   May I ask the gentleman a question?

MAGISTRATE. Yes—yes—you may ask him what questions you like.

JONES. Don't you remember you said you was a Liberal, same as your father, and you asked me wot I was?

JACK. [*With his hand against his brow*] I seem to remember——

JONES. And I said to you, "I'm a bloomin' Conserva*tive*," I said; an' you said to me, "You look more like one of these 'ere Socialists. Take wotever you like," you said.

JACK. [*With sudden resolution*] No, I don't. I don't remember anything of the sort.

JONES. Well, I do, an' my word's as good as yours. I've never been had up in a police court before. Look 'ere, don't you remember you had a sky-blue bag in your 'and——

[BARTHWICK *jumps.*

ROPER. I submit to your Worship that these questions are hardly to the point, the prisoner having admitted that he himself does not remember anything. [*There is a smile on the face of Justice.*] It is a case of the blind leading the blind.

JONES. [*Violently*] I've done no more than wot he 'as. I'm a poor man. I've got no money an' no friends—he's a toff—he can do wot I can't.

MAGISTRATE. Now, now! All this won't help you—you must be quiet. You say you took this box? Now, what made you take it? Were you pressed for money?

JONES. I'm always pressed for money.

MAGISTRATE. Was that the reason you took it?

JONES. No.

MAGISTRATE. [*To* SNOW] Was anything found on him?

SNOW. Yes, your Worship. There was six pounds twelve shillin's found on him, and this purse.

[*The red silk purse is handed to the* MAGISTRATE. BARTH-WICK *rises in his seat, but hastily sits down again.*

MAGISTRATE. [*Staring at the purse*] Yes, yes—let me see ——[*There is a silence.*] No, no, I've nothing before me as to the purse.. How did you come by all that money?

JONES. [*After a long pause, suddenly*] I declines to say.

MAGISTRATE. But if you had all that money, what made you take this box?

JONES. I took it out of spite.

MAGISTRATE. [*Hissing, with protruded neck*] You took it out of spite? Well now, that's something! But do you imagine you can go about the town taking things out of spite?

JONES. If you had my life, if you'd been out of work——

MAGISTRATE. Yes, yes; I know—because you're out of work you think it's an excuse for everything.

JONES. [*Pointing at* JACK] You ask 'im wot made 'im take the——

ROPER. [*Quietly*] Does your Worship require this witness in the box any longer?

MAGISTRATE. [*Ironically*] I think not; he is hardly profitable. [JACK *leaves the witness-box, and, hanging his head, resumes his seat.*

JONES. You ask 'im wot made 'im take the lady's——

[*But the* BALD CONSTABLE *catches him by the sleeve.*

BALD CONSTABLE. Sssh!

MAGISTRATE. [*Emphatically*] Now listen to me. I've nothing to do with what he may or may not have taken. Why did you resist the police in the execution of their duty?

JONES. It warn't their duty to take my wife, a respectable woman, that 'adn't done nothing.

MAGISTRATE. But I say it was. What made you strike the officer a blow?

JONES. Any man would a struck 'im a blow. I'd strike 'im again, I would.

MAGISTRATE. You are not making your case any better by violence. How do you suppose we could get on if everybody behaved like you?

JONES. [*Leaning forward, earnestly*] Well, wot about 'er; who's to make up to 'er for this? Who's to give 'er back 'er good name?

MRS. JONES. Your Worship, it's the children that's preying

on his mind, because of course I've lost my work. And I've had to find another room owing to the scandal.

MAGISTRATE. Yes, yes, I know—but if he hadn't acted like this nobody would have suffered.

JONES. [*Glaring round at* JACK] I've done no worse than wot 'e 'as. Wot I want to know is wot's goin' to be done to '*im*.

[*The* BALD CONSTABLE *again says* "*Hssh!*"

ROPER. Mr. Barthwick wishes it known, your Worship, that considering the poverty of the prisoners he does not press the charge as to the box. Perhaps your Worship would deal with the case as one of disorder.

JONES. I don't want it smothered up, I want it all dealt with fair—I want my rights——

MAGISTRATE. [*Rapping his desk*] Now you have said all you have to say, and you will be quiet. [*There is a silence; the* MAGISTRATE *bends over and parleys with his* CLERK.] Yes, I think I may discharge the woman. [*In a kindly voice he addresses* MRS. JONES, *who stands unmoving with her hands crossed on the rail.*] It is very unfortunate for you that this man has behaved as he has. It is not the consequences to him but the consequences to you. You have been brought here twice, you have lost your work—[*He glares at* JONES] and this is what always happens. Now you may go away, and I am very sorry it was necessary to bring you here at all.

MRS. JONES. [*Softly*] Thank you very much, your Worship.

[*She leaves the dock, and looking back at* JONES, *twists her fingers and is still.*

MAGISTRATE. Yes, yes, but I can't pass it over. Go away, there's a good woman. [MRS. JONES *stands back. The* MAGISTRATE *leans his head on his hand; then raising it, he speaks to* JONES.] Now, listen to me. Do you wish the case to be settled here, or do you wish it to go before a Jury?

JONES. [*Muttering*] I don't want no Jury.

MAGISTRATE. Very well then, I will deal with it here. [*After a pause.*] You have pleaded guilty to stealing this box——

JONES. Not to stealin'——

BALD CONSTABLE.   Hssshh.

MAGISTRATE.   And to assaulting the police——

JONES.   Any man as was a man——

MAGISTRATE.   Your conduct here has been most improper. You give the excuse that you were drunk when you stole the box.   I tell you that is no excuse.   If you choose to get drunk and break the law afterwards you must take the consequences. And let me tell you that men like you, who get drunk and give way to your spite or whatever it is that's in you, are—are—a *nuisance to the community.*

JACK.   [*Leaning from his seat*] Dad! that's what you said to me?

BARTHWICK.   Tsst.

[*There is a silence, while the* MAGISTRATE *consults his* CLERK; JONES *leans forward waiting.*

MAGISTRATE.   This is your first offence, and I am going to give you a light sentence.   [*Speaking sharply, but without expression.*]   One month with hard labour.

[*He bends, and parleys with his* CLERK.   *The* BALD CON-STABLE *and another help* JONES *from the dock.*

JONES.   [*Stopping and twisting round*] Call this justice? What about 'im?   'E got drunk!   'E took the purse—'e took the purse but [*in a muffled shout*] it's *'is money* got *'im* off—*Justice!*

[*The prisoner's door is shut on* JONES, *and from the seedy-looking men and women comes a hoarse and whispering groan.*

MAGISTRATE.   We will now adjourn for lunch!   [*He rises from his seat.*

[*The Court is in a stir.   ROPER gets up and speaks to the reporter.   JACK, throwing up his head, walks with a swagger to the corridor;* BARTHWICK *follows.*

MRS. JONES.   [*Turning to him with a humble gesture*] Oh! Sir!——

[BARTHWICK *hesitates, then yielding to his nerves, he makes a shamefaced gesture of refusal, and hurries out of Court.*   MRS. JONES *stands looking after him.*

                    The curtain falls.

JOHN GALSWORTHY

1867—1933

IN John Galsworthy's earlier years no one could possibly have seen in him a world-famous author or indeed any kind of writer at all. Yet he became one of the most outstanding English novelists and dramatists of his time, and received the highest national and international honours. Moreover there was nothing vulgar in his remarkable success story, for he remained all his life unself-seeking, modest and generous, a humane influence in British and international affairs.

John Galsworthy (he pronounced it *Gollsworthy*) was born at Kingston, near London, on August 14th, 1867, the son of a wealthy London solicitor and property owner, the original of Old Jolyon in *The Forsyte Saga*, whose ancestors were small farmers in Devonshire. John was educated at Harrow, one of the most famous and exclusive of English public schools, where he was Captain of Football, and at New College, Oxford, where he studied law. He went on to Lincoln's Inn, one of the ancient legal societies in London which maintain the standards of legal qualifications and conduct, and in 1890 he was called to the Bar, that is, he qualified as a barrister, who could conduct cases in the higher courts of law. He had no need to earn his living and he never practised law, but no doubt the legal training strengthened his natural tendency to judicious impartiality of mind and precision in the use of words. It is equally significant that he was born and grew up in the nineteenth century heyday of British prosperity, when the progress of civilization seemed assured and such barbarous catastrophes as the two world wars were unthinkable. John Galsworthy, a well-to-do young man about town, complete even to a monocle, seemed destined to remain shut up in that self-satisfied, comfortable little world to which most of the characters in his novels and plays belong.

An aimless social existence did not long appeal to him, however. He travelled adventurously in the Pacific and the Far East, and on the voyage home he met Joseph Conrad, the Polish seaman who became a great English novelist and Galsworthy's lifelong friend. He met other people who unsettled him. He began to discover the dreadful London slums of that time, from some of which his father drew rents, and he was horrified by what he found. The hypocrisy of his own class became intolerable to him. Most disturbing of all he fell deeply in love with his cousin's exceptionally beautiful and talented wife, Ada Galsworthy, who was very unhappy in her marriage. For ten years they maintained a secret love affair, often travelling abroad together. In those days a divorce was a major social sensation and Galsworthy's father would have been deeply distressed by it, so the lovers waited until after his death. They were married in 1905, and John Galsworthy remained devoted to Ada all his life. Some people thought him slavishly devoted.

Because she had been divorced she was shunned by most of their acquaintances, and it was this, coming when he was already deeply unsettled, which finally made Galsworthy rebel against the social class to which he belonged, while it was she who made him into a writer. Although there was no evidence at all except her own intuition, she was absolutely convinced of his latent ability, and reluctant as he was he could not refuse her anything. She helped and encouraged him constantly for the rest of his life. They discussed every detail of his work, and she typed nearly all of it herself, often three times over, for he revised everything meticulously. When he was writing with difficulty nothing helped him so much as her playing to him; she was a fine pianist and they both loved music.

His first book was a volume of feeble and imitative short stories, *From the Four Winds*, published in 1897. This was a failure in every way, and other failures followed, but the tide began to turn with his third novel *The Island Pharisees* (1904); and his fourth, *The Man of Property* (1906) was the first of his chronicles of the Forsyte family. Some people think it is his best work. He published nineteen novels between 1900 and 1933, besides many short stories, but his fame rests mainly on the numerous Forsyte novels and stories, which were collected as *The Forsyte Saga* (1922), *A Modern Comedy* (1929) and *End of the Chapter* (1935), and which achieved such an immense success on television nearly forty years later. Fastidiously written, like all his work, the early Forsyte novels show Galsworthy's shrewd observation of the class against which he had rebelled, the rich merchants who then governed Britain and who were sometimes so possessed by their love of money and property that as human beings they were destroyed by it. But the later novels, in which he arraigned the young people of the nineteen-twenties, sentimentalized the older Forsytes into much less unsympathetic figures. In fact the youthful rebel became the elderly conservative, as rebels so often do, but not before his writings and personal influence had contributed valuably to the movement towards greater social justice.

The novels show also his compassionate sympathy for the poor and oppressed, although he never understood them as well as he understood the rich. It is a powerful sympathy, which shows most clearly in his plays, many of which, from *The Silver Box* (1906) onwards, are clearly the work of a social reformer. He wrote twenty full-length plays and a number of short ones, and published also numerous volumes of verse, essays and lectures.

As his fame and popularity grew he mellowed into the eminent and widely respected man of letters. He and his wife were well received everywhere. He refused a knighthood, but accepted a distinguished British honour, the Order of Merit, in 1929, and honorary doctorates from many universities. He was awarded the Nobel Prize for Literature in 1932, and characteristically he gave the prize money to the P.E.N., the international fellowship of writers of which he was the first President. It still flourishes, and its objects are still those so dear to Galsworthy's heart: "to promote the friendly co-operation of writers in every country in the interests of literature, freedom of expression and international goodwill."

Apart from an interlude of hospital work, with his wife, during the First World War (and he loathed war), Galsworthy lived the quiet life of a successful man of letters who loved dogs and horses and worked hard. He usually gave away half his income, and he lived on a modest scale in London, Devonshire and elsewhere, but he and Ada travelled very widely about the world, mainly at her instigation. His large and continuous literary output and his travels would have been more than enough for most men, but all through his working life he gave much of his time to social and political causes, among them slum clearance, a minimum wage for workers in "sweated" industries, reforms in the divorce law and the prison system, votes for women, improvements in slaughter houses, and better working conditions for ponies in mines. The help which he gave privately to innumerable people in need was never publicized.

He died at Grove Lodge, Hampstead, in north London, on January 31st, 1933.

THE SILVER BOX

THE year 1906 was a landmark in John Galsworthy's career as a writer. On 23 March *The Man of Property* was published, the first of the series which became the famous *Forsyte Saga*, and possibly his best novel. It sold only about 5,000 copies, but it gave him for the first time (he had been writing for eleven years) an important place among the serious novelists of the day. And then on 25 September 1906, a few weeks after his thirty-ninth birthday, his first play, *The Silver Box*, was produced at the Court Theatre, London, to become at once the most discussed and controversial play of the year. The climate of opinion was beginning to change in his favour; the national conscience was stirring, and the Liberal Government, which had been elected in 1905, was beginning its great programme of social and political reforms.

Galsworthy's friend Edward Garnett had suggested to him in 1905 that he should write a play; he began it that winter at Bolt Head in Devonshire and he finished it in Kensington, London, in March 1906.

From the first it was intended for the Court Theatre, London, which was then making theatrical history—just as, fifty years later, it made history again, with John Osborne's *Look Back in Anger*. The series of new plays produced at the Court Theatre from 1904 to 1907, and brilliantly directed by J. E. Vedrenne and Harley Granville-Barker, was a landmark: it included plays by Shaw, Yeats, Granville-Barker, Gilbert Murray, Masefield and Galsworthy, and it began the modern era of English drama.

So many "plays of ideas" have been written since that we take them for granted, but in 1906 they were revolutionary, and often resented, for audiences of those days had long been accustomed to artificial plays written solely for light entertainment, with little truth to life and little artistic quality.

This theatrical revolution was not limited to Britain, it was European, and the two great leaders were the Norwegian, Henrik Ibsen (1828–1906), whose plays were translated into many languages, including English, and the Irishman, George Bernard Shaw (1856–1950), whose plays also were widely translated, but John Galsworthy followed with a distinctively English, although less substantial, contribution. His plays too were widely translated.

The Silver Box showed that a new dramatist had appeared, with a style and attitude of his own. His aim, as he said later himself, was "to create such an illusion of actual life passing on the stage as to compel the spectator to pass through an experience of his own, to think and talk and move with the people he sees thinking and talking and moving in front of him". Moreover Galsworthy gave the audience something important to think and talk about, a social problem or a question of conscience.

Many well-known people approved of this first play of his, from the famous actor-manager, Sir Herbert Beerbohm Tree, to H. G. Wells, H. W. Hudson and other leading writers. "Really good," was H. G. Wells's verdict, although he disliked Galsworthy's novels. The response of the Press was enthusiastic. Notices appeared in nearly sixty newspapers and magazines and only a very few were unfavourable. The dramatic critic of *The Times* concluded, "Our stage realists . . . are so rare and so valuable that we would not say a word to discourage a recruit to their little band so promising as Mr. John Galsworthy." *The Academy* said, "Mr. Galsworthy's scenes and his dialogue and his characters are startlingly effective . . . His technique is therefore impeccable. It is not...the technique of Ibsen. It is the technique of Mr. Galsworthy, who, probably by dint of not thinking about the matter at all, has evolved a method of his own for presenting life on the stage that is completely successful. Of course I do not mean that Mr. Galsworthy took no trouble with the construction of his play. That would be absurd . . . On the contrary *The Silver Box* is obviously built up by the most delicate strokes and is the product of the most careful and meticulous workman-ship. But when its author wrote it he was thinking of life, not of the theatre, and though he never forgot that he was writing for performance, he never allowed himself to sacrifice truth to mere stage effect or to shirk the situation as it would happen in life for the situation that the old-fashioned play-wright had found to be effective on the stage. Hence the extraordinary success of his play."

It was not a commercial success, in London or in New York; it did not draw large audiences. His first commercial success was his twelfth play, *The Skin Game*, fourteen years later. But Galsworthy (with others) went on writing serious plays. Besides some shorter pieces, he wrote twenty full-length plays between 1906 and 1926, among the most notable being *The Silver Box* (1906), *Strife* (1909), *Justice* (1910), *Loyalties* (1922) and *Escape* (1926). They established him as one of the leading dramatists of the time, and it was through his plays rather than his novels that he exercised his strongest influence for social reform. He was always more artist than reformer, however, and was rather aggrieved if his plays were valued more highly as propaganda than as drama. Years later he wrote in the collected edition of his works, "A dramatist [he means himself] strongly and pitifully impressed by the encircling pressure of modern environments . . . will not write plays detached from the movements and problems of his times. He is not conscious however of any desire to solve those problems in his plays or to effect great reforms. His only ambition in drama, as in his other work, is to present truth as he sees it and, gripping with it his readers or his audience, to produce in them a sort of mental and moral ferment, whereby vision may be enlarged, imagination livened and understanding promoted."

This was his aim in *The Silver Box*, written more than three-quarters of a century ago. It is for the reader or spectator of today to decide how far he has succeeded.

HOW FAR HAVE WE UNDERSTOOD?

POINTS FOR DISCUSSION AND COMPOSITION

ACT I, SCENE I

1. Is this an effective opening scene, likely to win the attention of the audience and put them into the right mood for what is to follow?

2. What is the point of the talk about political parties?

3. What have you learned from this scene and what do you now expect the play to be about?

ACT I, SCENE II

4. What kind of woman is Mrs. Jones? What have you learned from her about her husband and her attitude to him?

ACT I, SCENE III

5. Again there is talk of politics. What is the point of it here?

6. What dramatic purpose is served by the visit of the Unknown Lady? What, if anything, would the play lose if she did not appear?

7. What reasons has Barthwick for suspecting Mrs. Jones? Would you have suspected her if you had been in his place?

8. "Incidentally a butler, he is first a man," says Galsworthy of Marlow. In what way, if at all, has Marlow lived up to this description?

ACT II, SCENE I

9. Write a short conversation between Jones and another unemployed man who is looking for work, *or* between Jones and the barmaid at the "Goat and Bells." A third character may be introduced of you wish.

10. What do you think of Snow's behaviour in this scene?

11. "He's not a bad man, really," says Mrs. Jones of her husband. What can be said for and against this view?

Act II, Scene II

12. How does Mrs. Barthwick treat her son in this scene and in Act I, Scene III?

13. When and how does Galsworthy use for dramatic effect the contrast between the Jones' conditions and the Barthwicks'?

14. Compare Mrs. Jones with Mrs. Barthwick.

Act III

15. Why does Galsworthy bring in the two little girls?

16. Is this the most dramatic scene in the play? If not, which scene is?

17. Is Jack ashamed of himself or merely relieved to have escaped scot-free? What do you think of him now?

18. To what extent does Jack owe his escape to Roper?

19. Is Jones himself treated unfairly during the trial? If so, in what way?

20. Is the Magistrate's behaviour a conscious betrayal of justice?

21. Is Jones likely to be a better man or a worse when he comes out of prison? Should prisons be used to punish offenders or to reform them?

22. Which speech in this scene, if any, states the theme of the play?

GENERAL

23. Can *The Silver Box* be described as a play about two thefts?

24. Where and how does Galsworthy show that he is trying to be fair to his characters and to state both sides of the questions raised?

25. Barthwick talks about his principles. What are they and does he live up to them?

26. Which character do you regard as (*a*) most honourable; (*b*) most hypocritical; (*c*) most admirable; (*d*) most despicable; (*e*) most unreasonable; (*f*) most to be pitied? Justify your choice.

27. "The lower classes are their own enemies," says Barthwick. "If they would only trust us they would get on so much better" (Act II, Scene II). What do you think of this in the light of what happens in this play?

28. Do you agree or disagree with the Magistrate's judgment, and why?

29. Another playwright, Mr. St. John Ervine, said that all Galsworthy's characters were in the dock (on trial) or on the Judge's bench. What did he mean? How far is it true of the characters in *The Silver Box*?

30. Is Jones to blame for his fate?

31. When, if at all, do you like (*a*) Barthwick; (*b*) Mrs. Barthwick?

32. *The Silver Box* was produced at the Court Theatre by Harley Granville-Barker, a distinguished playwright, actor and producer and later a famous critic of Shakespeare. Before players were chosen Galsworthy wrote to him: "The keynote of Barthwick is *want of courage*. He thinks himself full of *principle* and invariably *compromises* in the face of facts. The keynote of Mrs. Barthwick is want of imagination. Her imagination is only once aroused and that by a *personal* touch, viz., by the child's crying at the end of Act II . . . Mrs. Barthwick is not more than fifty and well preserved. The keynote of Jack is inherent want of *principle* derived from Barthwick and courage *by fits and starts* derived from Mrs. Barthwick. The keynote of Jones is *smouldering revolt*. The keynote of Mrs. Jones is *passivity* and she must not be played pathetically, only *be* pathetic from force of circumstances . . . The solicitor is a combination of easy-going asthmatic stolidity with a quick-glancing rapidity of perception and speech . . . "Authors are by no means invariably right about their own work. How far do Galsworthy's views fit the characters as they appear to you?

33. Galsworthy's first title for *The Silver Box* was *The*

Cigarette Box. Which do you think is the better title, and why?

34. If you were acting in a production of the play which part would you like to take, and why?

35. When and by whom are the following words spoken, and what comments can you make on them?

(*a*) We're all equal before the law.

(*b*) If I were you I wouldn't live with him.

(*c*) The motor-cars are against him.

(*d*) I sometimes give them sixpence.

(*e*) The purse must be kept out of it.

(*f*) He says the whole story's stuff.

(*g*) Men like you are a nuisance to the community.

36. Write an additional scene in which Mrs. Jones comes to the Barthwicks and asks them to take her back.

37. Where does the climax of the play occur, the point of highest tension?

38. What are the chief differences between a play of this kind and a poetic play such as one of Shakespeare's?

39. Compare *The Silver Box* with Galsworthy's play, *Loyalties*, or with any other play about a theft.

40. Can you find any instances of Galsworthy's use of understatement for dramatic effect? Would strong emphasis have been more effective?

41. "Galsworthy revolutionized [British Drama] by his realism . . . Galsworthy's aim when he wrote *The Silver Box* was to produce a play throughout in which there should be no movement, no gesture, no word, no scene, no furniture that would not be there in real life if the fourth wall were removed from the rooms in which the play was staged, and at the same time, of course, so to select these movements, gestures, words, etc., that they brought out not merely scenes of everyday life but the essence of human nature in significant situations" —Leon Schalit: *John Galsworthy, A Survey,* 1929, page 228. How far has Galsworthy succeeded in his aim?

42. What have you learned about Galsworthy from *The Silver Box?*

ACTING NOTES

A PLAY is written to be performed, and the printed text, like a musical score, is simply the basis for a performance. When reading to himself the reader should hear and see everything, and the practised, imaginative reader can stage a good performance in his own mind; but drama is a communal art, and it is only as a combination of sound, movement and pictorial effect, presented to an audience, that a play can come fully to life.

Any group of people studying this play for their own purposes should attempt at least a half-performance, walking about book in hand, and rehearsing some if not all of the scenes by reading them several times and trying to make improvements every time. If the group wish to please an audience they should not choose this play for performance unless they can cast it fairly well, and in particular they must have players who can give acceptable renderings of Jones and his wife and Barthwick.

The group must also have a producer whose rulings they will accept and who will take charge of the production in much the same way as a conductor takes charge of an orchestra. The producer is responsible for the artistic harmony and unity of the play in all its details, and the success of the performance will depend largely on his knowledge, imagination, tact, enthusiasm, and willingness to learn.

When the play has been chosen, application for permission to perform it should be made *at once* to The Secretary, The Incorporated Society of Authors, 84 Drayton Gardens, London S.W.10, giving the name of the amateur company and the number, place and dates of the performances they wish to give.

The other business arrangements should also be started well in advance, booking the hall, finding printers for posters, tickets and programmes, getting lighting equipment, stage settings and so on. A detailed list of everything which has to be done should be made at a very early stage, and responsibilities should be allocated in writing.

Several auditions—trial readings—may be necessary before all the parts are finally cast, and before rehearsals can begin the producer must study the play very thoroughly, with his cast and stage in mind. He must see and hear clearly everything which happens. He should make himself a prompt-book, by breaking up two copies of the play and sticking the leaves on alternate pages of an exercise book. This gives him space for a stage-plan, or a series of stage-plans, for every scene, showing the position of furniture, doors, etc., and the entrances, movements, groupings, exits, etc., of the players, with notes on lighting, "noises off," etc. Since the play is the work of a very skilful and experienced playwright the author's stage-directions should be followed if they suit the stage to be used and the producer's interpretation of the play.

Every player should have a copy of the play for himself, so that he can study it as a whole, but he should not begin learning his part by heart until after the first rehearsals have been held and he has been shown his entrances, exits, and most important movements, so that he can associate these with words from the start. He must then learn his part, and cues, as quickly as possible. If the rehearsals are not held on the stage, a plan of the stage must be marked out on the floor of the rehearsal room; otherwise the change to the stage may confuse movements and groupings very badly.

The Silver Box is obviously a realistic play which would gain from realistic settings, and these are not numerous or difficult. The play can, however, be given quite successfully in a curtain setting. This is much better than unconvincing attempts at realism and long waits for scene-changing, which do great damage to a performance. It would be an advantage, but it is not essential, to have two sets of curtains; a very shabby set for the Joneses' room in Act II, Scene I, which may perhaps be used also, if it can be smartened up, for Act III; and another set, dark blue or green or brown, for the Barthwicks' house.

Lighting is always important, but *The Silver Box* gives little scope for subtlety or variation. The depression of Act II, Scene I, should be accentuated by dimmer lighting, but (as in all scenes) it must be bright enough for faces to be clearly seen from the back of the hall. Headlights and footlights must be adjusted to eliminate unwanted shadows.

In *The Silver Box*, as in most plays, scene-changing and lighting rehearsals are essential if mistakes, delays and noise are to avoided.

Costumes of 1906 are almost essential; Edwardian England belongs to the past as surely as Victorian England. At least the attempt to suggest the costumes should be made. Any good library may have magazines of the time, such as *The Illustrated London News* and *Punch*, and there are numerous illustrated histories and biographies covering the period.

But it is the acting which makes or ruins the performance. The players are very unlikely to be great actors but they can learn in rehearsal some of the rudiments of good acting. They must be word-perfect in their parts. (There should be, however, a reliable prompter in a strategic position during the last few rehearsals and during the performances). Every word must be clearly audible at the back of the hall—which is secured by clear articulation, not by shouting. Cues must be taken promptly. (Slowness in taking cues is one of the commonest and most fatal defects of amateur acting.) Every player must know and understand the play as a whole, and must act every minute he is on the stage, no matter how small his part may be. When he has nothing to say or do he must continue to be the character he represents; he must react, although not always visibly, to everything which happens, remembering always that this character never knows what is going to happen next; it is only the player who knows that.

It is for the producer to give every scene a dramatic shape.